On a pig's back

Also by
John Holgate in Pan Books
Make a cow laugh

John Holgate

On a pig's back

Life on a small farm

Pan Books London and Sydney

First published 1978 by Peter Davies Limited
This edition published 1979 by Pan Books Ltd,
Cavaye Place, London SW10 9PG
© John Holgate 1978
ISBN 0 330 25781 1
Set, printed and bound in Great Britain by
Cox & Wyman Ltd, Reading

for Johanna, Michael and Naomi
— so that they may be mentioned

Contents

1	The great cow chase	9
2	An early morning affair	15
3	Goodbye to Alice Capone	19
4	Wild geese and goslings	24
5	Feeding the growing grass	28
6	Paulina and a potent after-shave	34
7	Early grass and a late arrival	39
8	Cabbage plants and sowing	44
9	A bit of muck for luck	49
10	Jumping about with pigs	55
11	Enter Percy Pig	61
12	May Day and may blossom	66
13	The cattle trade collapses	72
14	Haymaking in the rain	78
15	The season's task – shearing	85
16	A woolly lawn-mower	92
17	Birds' eggs and porky picnickers	95
18	The bovine mammary gland	99
19	A left-handed cow and a bumblefoot	104
20	A prickly problem	111
21	A crisis with our milk	115
22	Warbles and Rufus goes blind	120
23	Everything goes to the Fund	125
24	Cashing lambs and a hobbling ewe	133
25	Bringing home the barley	140
26	The epic of Chanticleer	147
27	The rams run out	150
28	Annie Pig's tale	154
29	A threadbare countryside	158
30	A ewe is killed by dogs	163
31	The eve of Christmas and a calf	166

1 The great cow chase

The great cow chase, alias the Holgate Stakes, inaugurated our new farming year. It was an impromptu affair raced over a course which covered most of Egerton's seventy-five acres. Dairy cows came first and second, I ran a fairly creditable third, and Shirley, my wife, ended an hysterical fourth.

It happened the last week in March and took place because our neighbour was renting a prize Hereford bull and because Nitpicker, one of our dairy cows, was not in calf.

This was entirely in keeping with her character. If there was a way of doing something wrong, no matter what, she found it. What was easy for the rest of the herd was to her a brain-bursting problem. The slightest deviation from routine shattered her.

For example, the collecting yard, where the cows were brought twice daily, was connected with the milking parlour by a sliding door. Nitpicker invariably came through the door with a rush which carried her across the intervening space to the third of the six stands. Alas, should this place be occupied, she was completely flummoxed. Any other animal would move to where there was a vacancy – but not her! A few moments of panic and back she rushed into the collecting yard pushing aside any incoming cow to begin all over again. The result was chaos.

This being her nature, it was not surprising that while we had managed to get other cows in calf by using the Artificial Insemination Service, it had not been successful with her.

The need to do so arose from the fact that cows produce milk to feed calves, not to fill bottles for housewives. Furthermore, the multi-stomached bovines come on heat for only three days every three weeks and are not fertile for all of the seventy-two hours. When a calf is born the cow begins a lactation period of some 305 days and then goes dry. No new calf, no more milk. It is as simple as that.

Nitpicker had been visited three times by the AI officials but had not 'taken'. The answer, our rustic friends agreed, was a 'natural' bull. 'They've bin doing it a lot longer than the bowler-hatted gentlemen,' our nearest neighbour, fair-haired, thick-set Willem, told us 'Bring her down to my place and let's see what that bull can do!' He added a caution. 'Them cows have been shedded since before Christmas so she might be a bit frisky. Better walk her along with another, they'm always easier to handle when there's two or more.'

That figured: we had read all about the herd instinct in the textbooks which supplied most of our farming knowledge. What better companion for her than the sober-sided Gaffer, the boss cow of our little herd?

Next morning, after the kids had gone to school, Shirley and I went over to the covered yard and separated the two animals from their herd mates. They could hardly believe their big, brown eyes when they saw the open gate: freedom after months of restraint! They needed no urging.

Our troubles began immediately they were in the open. They kicked up their heels like bucking broncos and took off ... in the wrong direction! The field gates had been left open to allow the sheep the free run of the farm in the winter months. The cows shot through the first one like leather rockets, everything working, tails, udders, hips, horns, heads, the lot!

In retrospect we should have been cool, calm and collected, but perhaps the cows' mood was infectious. Shirley was handicapped by multi-layers of woollies, not the best of racing gear. She looked like a knitted doll. I had a polo-necked sweater; one she had made with wool half an inch thick to judge by the heat it generated. But, instinctively, without pausing to think, both of us hared after the runaways, closing gates as we went. Down they galloped at a furious pace to the bottom fields where a stream marked our boundary, then left, anti-clockwise, bringing them to the Plough Field, through the Twelve-Acre and back into the House Field where it had all begun.

It was a fair test of stamina in conditions where frozen ground was beginning to thaw into slush. My legs were like lead. Shirley's began to bend like rubber.

The cows would have gone round again but now they were restricted to the House Field. The rest of the herd crowded excitedly at the yard rails and bellowed encouragement to them. Our salvation came when the pair charged up to their friends. Shirley summoned her reserves and got the gate open and I shooed the pair into the yard. Neither of us spoke; we simply walked silently into the house to have a cup of coffee and recover.

'There never was anything like this in suburbia,' my wife wailed as her breath came back. 'Thursday morning was coffee with Janet.'

I tried to console her. 'You ran very well, dear. In London I doubt if you could have lasted even half the course.'

'Big deal!' she sniffed and went straight to the telephone and called the AI service. They promised to come in the afternoon and this time the service was successful. Perhaps the gallop did the trick.

Naturally we had to tell Willem why the cow had not arrived. It proved that, much to his delight, he had witnessed most of the great chase.

'My word, Jacky, you was going well when you come through the Plough Field,' he said with well-feigned admiration. 'I'd have laid money on you then but I think the going was too soft. Them cows began to pull away when you all turned for home.'

Just as naturally, the story of the Holgate Stakes – as the incident became known – was manna to our friends in The Forge, the little pub which was the centre of the scattered community's social life.

'Here he comes,' the reigning spirit, Old Jonathon, chuckled when I walked in the following evening. 'They tells me you got into the prize money but the Missus didn't get a place.'

He looked smaller, more fragile and more gnome-like than ever. He had been missing from his seat by the fire for nearly a week having been poorly and confined to his house. It was nice to see him out again and his twinkling eyes robbed his teasing of malice. Jonathon put a high value on friendship but could never resist starting an argument.

'Racing is one way of keeping cows warm in this cold weather,' the genial Griff who hosted the pub said, raising his bushy fly-away eyebrows.

The Forge was a quiet place at this time of the year except

when the darts team was playing at home. Mostly, the locals – Griff's faithfuls – had it to themselves. The townees who rediscovered it every summer were still locked in their centrally heated cities.

Howard, the stocky, down-to-earth ex-infantry sergeant who had befriended us from the start of our farming venture, supped beer and declared, 'They'm a sensible lot. What kind of idiot wants to scrape a living farming when you can do better sitting on your fat backside in a warm, comfortable office?'

Griff looked at me, read my thoughts, and laughed. It was what we were trying to do.

'They'm out all hours of the day and night dining and dancing, it's all furs and pockets stuffed with money for them,' Old Jonathon announced. 'No wonder the country's going to ruin.'

He was a telly addict. His view of the 'outside' world depended on what programme he had last seen.

'It's not really like that,' I ventured, but he was in full flight.

'Nah, I remember you and the Missus' – the title always made Shirley wince when she heard it – 'coming in through that door the first time, dressed like toffs, green as grass, rattling on about being farmers, daft as brushes. I'll bet, if you'd knowed what you was taking on, you'd uv turned tail and run for it.'

Griff's instinctive courtesy brought him in on my side. 'Don't regret it, do you Jacky?'

Old Jonathon was unrelenting. 'If you don't then the frost must have got into your head through the cracks. Getting out of bed at five o'clock to milk cows, mucking out pigs, up to your bottom in snow and sludge. No regrets! You ain't that daft.'

'Leave him be,' said his brother Matthew, who suffered badly from back trouble in the cold weather we were having. 'Stop your damn needling folks. You'm making me feel bad. What's the matter with you? Lack of sin or feeling your age?'

'Let me get some drinks,' I said and collected the glasses.

As ever, The Forge was immaculate. It never ceased to amaze me how Griff and his happy-faced wife managed it. No matter how foul the weather, the red-tiled floor seldom showed a trace of the heavy working boots that tramped across it. The horse-brasses and copper ornaments which stood on the high mantelpiece or hung from wooden pegs driven into the rough, white-painted stone walls always looked freshly polished as they blinked in the firelight. It was like some granny's parlour with the comforting knowledge that, no matter who you were, what you wanted, whether you wiped your feet or not, you were always welcome.

At one time The Forge had been the blacksmith's shop for the district. The heavy, stomping farmhorses had been brought here, and while they were being shod their owners would take a few tankards of the strong, black, treacly beer the smith brewed in another part of the long, low building. It was potent stuff and many a man, over-estimating his own capacity, had been lifted on to a broad back and the horse sent off with a slap to find its own way home.

Nowadays the workhorses had gone, replaced by tractors. There were petrol and diesel pumps in the forecourt, a café served snacks for the passing motor trade, and a large freezer compartment provided ice-cream and the like for local children and convenience foods for busy country housewives. Even so, in some subtle way that defied explanation, The Forge remained a 'farmers' pub'.

This was most marked when livestock sales were held in the small hill market across the road. Then the place would be crowded with shrewd-eyed dealers and farmers from richer, lower farms, looking to pick up hardy young stock reared in the immediate vicinity of the pub or, better still, brought down from the remote holdings high up on the peaked mountain which dominated our own little farm and the whole area. On such occasions Griff, his wife and their family helpers were hard pushed to keep pace with the demand for ale to soothe throats and tempers roughened by hard bargaining and prices which did not please everyone.

That evening, walking home, it was hard to believe that it was little more than a year ago that a fat, middle-aged suburbanite, his wife and their family had come rattling and rolling in two vehicles down this same lane, intent on changing the comforts of London's commuterland for the unknown trials, tribulations and triumphs of farming. So much had happened since then.

The ground crunched under my boots. It had been frosty too that first day. Shirley and the two youngest, Vicky, pigtails and rosy cheeks, 'going ten' now, and Nicholas Paul, nearly five years younger, blond, stocky and perpetually hungry, had travelled in the family car, an 1800. Our older son John, just seventeen, intent on making a career in farming, and myself had been in Old Lil, the scruffy diesel van bought from a dealer in the Lewisham area of London.

Old Jonathon was nearer to the truth than he guessed. Had any of us known just what lay ahead, we might well have about-turned and run. In truth, by the time our little cavalcade had arrived at Egerton that day, we were committed. Buying the farm had emptied our pockets and there was no going back. Our problem had been how to learn quickly enough to survive; we had managed that – just. Providence, they say, cares for fools. It might well be true but we also owed a lot to the friends we had made, especially the men I had just left.

It was a cold, still night. On my right hand the moonlight flickered over the gentle mounds covering a buried Saxon village; while far away in the other direction, below me, over the saddle of the mountain, the sky was garish – white and yellow – with the lights of half a dozen Midland towns.

The grass in the fields, the hedgerows and the trees were frost-white. The pond was frozen over with a cloth of ice like the finest lace flung over the water. There was no sound or sign of life from the pens and stalls; our animals were sleeping.

I found Shirley sitting ready by the fire in the main living-room. She was a small, trim woman in dressing-gown and sheep-skin slippers. Her auburn hair, newly washed, was gathered in a towel turban. It was remarkable how she managed to cope with a hundred and one household chores; organize and feed a ravenous, extrovert family; bottle, cook or freeze just about everything that grew in field or garden; nurse calves, piglets and lambs; and still look as cool and neat as freshly laundered linen.

'Did you see Howard?' she asked. My visit to The Forge had not been completely for pleasure. 'How's everyone?'

'Old Jonathon's had flu. He seemed a bit depressed.'

She padded into the kitchen to make coffee. 'Poor little man.

He's got no one to look after him. It's all this waiting for the better weather. If we could just see the sun, I'm sure everything would improve.'

For Shirley, Hell was a cold place.

2 An early morning affair

Next morning, my enemy, the alarm-clock, dragged me out of sleep and made me surrender a warm bed at five o'clock. Every day began with the same battle, every day I lost. The cows had to be milked; there was no one else to do it. I sat on the edge of the bed and dressed hurriedly.

Ours was an old house. Some parts of it dated back 400 years and there had probably been other, earlier dwellings on the same site. It had a friendly atmosphere, as if it wore a wry, sympathetic smile. A lot of men before me had stumbled, drugged with sleep, down the narrow stairs to begin their labours.

When I stepped through the door into the wakening day, the land was brittle with a frost that had magicked rank grass and the tall wrack of weed and foxglove into things of beauty. The big ash in the garden was its masterpiece.

My lady friend – Miss Tinkerbell, the cat – was waiting, as ever, on the garden wall. As I opened the gate she climbed on to my shoulder, nuzzled her greeting and pushed inside the cowl of the old duffel coat to lie across my back like a warm, living scarf and ride over to the milking parlour.

Nominally she belonged to my daughter who had carried her home one afternoon after tea with a school friend. At that stage there had not been much more than a scrap of fur, a pink mouth and a mew. Her mother had died after giving birth to the litter and although the girl and her mother had tried to rear them all, only Miss Tinkerbell had survived. The fuss and indulgence had inspired a self-confidence bordering on arrogance.

15

From the moment of her arrival, Egerton had belonged to her. Like many other decorative females, she considered, with some justification, that every other creature there – biped or quadruped – was privileged to be her slave.

There had been a scheme in the beginning to make her into a house-cat. After all she was a striking tortoiseshell with yellow-green eyes, perfect colouring to go with our best London carpet. Shirley was much in favour but this house-cat business was not to Miss Tinkerbell's liking. No, sir! She endured it for four days. On the fifth she stepped outside, ignored the frenzied threats of the tethered collie and, tail erect, went on a tour of the buildings.

Barney the Bastard Barncat, a big, black and white neutered Tom, appeared from his barn and introduced himself to her, only to be treated with a contempt that reduced him to grovelling. He followed the petite newcomer around, mewing protests in his cracked-plate voice, but continued to be totally and absolutely ignored.

At the end of her inspection Miss Tinkerbell had decided that this was for her. None of the 'what a pretty cat stretched out on the carpet' nonsense. Thereafter, although she was repeatedly carried indoors, she rarely stayed more than an hour or two. She found a warm corner in the foodstore and moved in.

There was a vacancy for a dairy cat. Our London moggy, Fanny Fatcat, had died from poison, possibly picked up from rats, shortly before the kitten's arrival. Barney was too nervous and upset the cows. It was tailor-made for Miss Tinkerbell. She was quite at ease with cows, did not alarm them, and never objected when they tried to taste her fur.

She evolved a routine and stuck to it. It began with our morning meeting. Once in the milking parlour, she let me get on with my work and took up a position by a battered old aluminium dish which was known as 'the begging bowl'. It was a well-paid post. The cows' teats were checked by milking a few drops into a stripping cup before the units were put on. This went into the bowl. In addition John – who helped me in the evenings and when he was on holiday – and I always marked the end of the milking session by pouring her a small libation. In very quick time she developed into a sleek, plump cat.

Her life was not entirely without alarms and excursions. There was one dreadful moment when a cow, Lizzie-three-spot, accidentally trod on her. Trapped under the big hoof, the kitten screeched helplessly. The cow could feel nothing. It was only by thumping her on the leg with the begging bowl that we got her to lift the foot. Miss Tinkerbell shot out of the parlour as if she was jet-propelled. Happily no lasting damage was done and the next morning she was waiting on the garden wall, showing her fortitude by reporting back for duty.

In return for the perks and privileges of her position Miss Tinkerbell kept the dairy and the milking parlour free from the mice which were attracted by the tasty concentrates – dairy nuts – fed to the cows. She took her duties extremely seriously and most mornings, usually while I was setting up the milking tackle, she went round the walls feeling in any cracks and crevices where a scheming mouse might try to hide. It was astonishing how often she dragged out some poor hapless rodent. They were mercilessly dispatched but never eaten until the milking was completed. Then, as I did the washing and tidying, she carried them off to some secret dining spot.

It often seemed to me that somewhere along the line we had gone wrong with our cows. Our neighbours had only to look in the direction of their animals and the four-legged milkbars rushed to comply with their masters' unspoken wishes. Not so ours.

There was no discernible reaction now when I appeared in the cow yard and shouted, as threateningly as possible, 'Heyup'. It seemed the appropriate thing to say.

There were sixteen of them, big black and white Friesians. We had preferred animals experienced enough and tolerant enough to forgive our early fumbling and blundering and, as a result, had ended up with this rather elderly, world-weary bunch.

Nothing we did surprised or impressed them. They had seen it all before. They lay in their various sleeping spots, endlessly chewing the cud – the most dominant got the warmest places – and hardly bothered to look up. One or two condescended to turn a bored head in my direction with a 'What on earth can he possibly want?' expression on their long, thin faces. The majority

17

ignored me, perhaps in the hope that I would go elsewhere.

There was nothing for it but to walk round and plant a foot on one or two backsides. It had to be done carefully, I had heard stories of angry farmers breaking toes.

They mostly held out until I actually lifted a foot and then got up reluctantly, stretched, curled their tails over their backs, defecated fluidly, and lurched forward. Each and every one of them knew precisely what was required but each and every morning we went through this same charade.

Once a few had moved the rest followed, resigned to beginning another day. The last cow out was always a big white animal, a Blue Friesian, Whitey. She was a prodigious producer but had trouble with her hips, perhaps a touch of arthritis like me. It took her a little time to overcome the inertia and get everything loose and moving. I helped by massaging her back.

One after another they scurried the twenty yards or so in the open to reach the sheltered collecting yard. It was a sobering thought that our economic survival largely depended on them. At this time of the year and this time of the day they were not an impressive sight. Their bed manners were not to be commended. They did not choose their sleeping spots well. Bits of straw and unspeakable matter clung to their coats. Lizzie, the cow that stood on the cat, and several others were ungainly with calf.

My biggest problem these days was cleaning dried muck off udders; not an occupation to be recommended before breakfast – or at any other time. A kitchen scourer would have been useful but I had to settle for a rag, warm water and patience. Cows, I had learned, do not like having sore teats and they are apt to emphasize their objections by applying a large splayed foot to whatever portion of the milker happens to be accessible. I was an experienced limper. This morning, by my standards, things went smoothly. By seven-thirty they were back in the yard, eating the hay spread in the feed racks, and the milk was ready to go to the stand at the top of the lane.

Next question-mark lay over Old Lil, the diesel van. She had been standing outside all night in the cold. Fortunately she was addicted to Quick Start aerosol fluid and could be bribed. A few whiffs produced a racking cough. The engine spat and spluttered but finally settled into a steady *pop-pop*. I loaded the churns and set out.

The Milk Marketing Board lorry came rattling up on cue and Jock, the stocky little driver, collected our offerings, replaced them with four empty churns, hazarded an opinion that the weather would get warmer and went to his next pick-up.

A few minutes later I was rolling in through the lane gate intent on breakfast. It was 8.10 when I sat down at the kitchen table, ravenously hungry.

Shirley was in a 'do you know' mood.

'Do you know that civilized people are just coming downstairs in every other part of the world?' she asked sweetly. 'Do you also know that, apart from Eskimos, we are the only family who wear Balaclava helmets round the house?'

I did not know these things and they were not true. She was the only one of the family who would wear a Balaclava indoors.

'Jock says it's going to get warmer,' I assured her. 'And you'll see, when things get easier, we'll put in central heating: three radiators in every room.'

'I believe you,' she said, making a face, 'but there are thousands of women who wouldn't.'

3 Goodbye to Alice Capone

Spring – and it was becoming bolder every morning – meant the growth of new grass, turning out the cattle, and livestock sales. For some weeks we had been reading advertisements in the local newspapers or posters stuck up in markets announcing special livestock sales.

Ours, although we were trying to make a living from dairying, was predominantly a stock-rearing area. Local farmers bought in young calves, reared them to yearlings, sometimes beyond, and sold them to others on softer, easier land to finish off for the fatstock markets.

Now was the time for us to cash in. Buyers were looking for stock to go out on the grass now coming through. We knew all this, but the animals we had ready for sale were Alice Capone and her mob. It was like selling family.

They were very different now from the stick-legged creatures brought to us by the calf dealer some twelve months previously. We had carried them from his van to the pens. In the intervening time they had grown into sleek black and white Friesian–Hereford heifers but they still regarded us as their friends. Shirley, who had borne the brunt of their 'milk' period, had only to appear and, whether they were in the pen or free in the fields, they would come up to be petted.

'I suppose they must go,' she said wistfully.

'The bank manager would consider that an unnecessary question,' I informed her.

'Probably,' she agreed. 'But these were our first calves.'

When the time came to phone the auctioneers in the nearby town and tell them to include the six in the sale catalogue, I felt like Judas.

The evening before the sale John and I curry-combed all of them but they needed little grooming. Their coats glistened and they looked healthy and plump. Victoria Jane and Nicholas Paul came along to say goodbye.

'What will happen to them now?' the five-year-old Nicholas asked.

'Who knows?' John said. 'They might be bought by someone who wants to use them for breeding.'

'Have calves of their own?'

'Something like that.'

We all prefer to evade reality when it is unpleasant. The kids were no exception.

Next morning when the cattle lorry arrived, Shirley remained indoors. She was not coming to the sale.

'They look a nice bunch,' the driver said as they went up the ramp made by dropping the tailboard of the big vehicle. 'They'm fetching a fair bit.'

'Let's hope so,' I told him. 'There's a lot gone into them.'

'Ah, I've had some of it myself. It takes work to get them ready,' he said heartily. But he misunderstood my meaning.

He set off for the town some seven or eight miles away while I went back indoors to get ready and follow him.

'You could go shopping,' I suggested, but Shirley chose to remain at home.

'Don't worry,' she said. 'I know they have to go, it's just that these were a little bit special.'

From The Forge it was downhill most of the way to the town. It was a cold, dry day. On either side of the road fields were beginning to flush green and there was the flash and glint of celandine and primrose in the sheltered hedgerows. Outside Ellis the Cowman's place six empty churns stood on the milkstand but there was no sign of the little man who had taught me the rudiments of dairying. Probably he was working round the back of the buildings.

When I arrived the market was buzzing with people, some familiar, some with an indefinable difference which singled them out as 'foreigners'. There was a Welsh lilt to the speech of many of the men who moved from pen to pen assessing the qualities of the cattle on offer and making notes on their catalogues. They had brought in stock from the high hill farms and were anxious to see how it compared with local products.

Alice Capone – she had earned the name by her aggressiveness as a young calf – and her friends had already been processed. They had averaged four-and-a-half hundredweight on the big market scales and had a round label giving their lot number as 37 stuck on their rumps. By comparison with some of the rough-coated, lean animals around them, they looked sturdy. A barrel-chested man in a tweed suit and flat hat was discussing them with two companions.

'They're about what we're looking for,' he said. 'They've had a better start than most here and good coats.'

'You won't beat them,' a voice said behind me while a big hand gripped my shoulder. 'This bloke here's brought them in and they've been running on top of a damn great big mountain up to their bellies in ice and snow.'

The speaker was Tall Stan, a friend whom I often met at sales.

'Have they though?' the thickset one said. 'Will he guarantee them?'

'Where would you be taking them?' Stan asked.

'Down south, Berkshire, to run on grass.'

The tall man laughed. 'Guarantee them down there? These girls will think they'm on holiday. They'll grow so fast, you'll never get them through the gates.'

The trio laughed. 'Well then, I suppose we'd better give them a bit of a go when they come up,' barrel-chest said, and they went off.

After they had left Tall Stan looked more carefully at the six. 'They don't look bad at all,' he said finally. 'Got anything else in the sale?'

'Just these, but they haven't been running on any mountain, Stan.'

'Never mind, they've been near enough,' he said grinning. 'Down south they'll put on weight like pigs. It's marshmallow country. You ought to make £70 on these. Don't take less.'

The sales ring was under cover with tiers of seats arranged in amphitheatre style. It was crowded by the time selling began. The auctioneer, a handsome, well-groomed man, Mark Boyce, often took the small Forge sales and when Alice and company were brought into the ring, I joined him in the box.

'Now there's a fine bunch,' he enthused. 'Not a bad one among them. They'll go on and make fine big animals. From right up among the mountains.'

I looked across the ring and saw barrel-chest lean over and say something to his friends. Tall Stan was a couple of rows behind them.

'Now what am I bid? Who'll start me? Say £70 a go?'

A slim young man said, '£60.'

My heart sank, but Boyce was unshaken. 'It's a beginning, nothing more, just a beginning. Now who'll say £65?'

To my astonishment Tall Stan nodded.

'£65, I'm bid. Now say £70?'

The Berkshire man held up two fingers.

'£67. Who'll even it up, make it £70?'

Tall Stan nodded. The Berkshire buyer looked round to see who was bidding.

The auctioneer stroked his nose. '£71?'

Barrel-chest waved his catalogue.

The slim young man joined in again and I saw Tall Stan grin. He did not bid again but between them the other two took the price up to £79 in single pound bids. It ended with barrel-chest in possession.

The auctioneer brought matters to a conclusion. 'Selling once, selling twice, last chance, I sell to Mr Trowbridge at £79.'

His gavel thumped on the table-top in front of him.

Alice and friends no longer belonged to us! They were ushered out of the ring to await collection.

'You'd better buy Stan a beer or two,' Boyce told me with a smile tugging at his mouth. 'Tell him, if he wants, I'll lend him the hammer next time.'

He turned to the next batch: Lot 38. 'Now there's a fine bunch of cattle . . .'

'That's a good price,' Tall Stan said when I joined him. 'But they was a nice little lot.'

'Thanks for the help, but what would you have done if no one else had bid?'

'At £65? Bought them of course, if you'd been daft enough to sell. But I thought they'd go over £70.'

He walked with me to the market office to collect the cheque and then to take a last look at the six. Beauty and Black Eye, they all had names, came to the rails when I called them. Shirley had lavished care and affection on the bunch from the moment they arrived on Egerton as long-legged, bawling babies, our very first livestock.

'The wife's pets,' I explained rather shamefacedly. 'You know how women are about calves.'

'There can't be pets in farming, Jacky, you can't afford to have them,' he said, not deceived.

He declined my offer of beer and settled for a cup of tea in the cafeteria. I offered him a £1 note for 'luck' but he laughed and refused. 'Never mind. You'll be able to do something for me one of these days.'

Shirley was baking cakes to go into the deep freeze when I got home. Something to take her mind off the sale, I suspected.

'Did it go all right?' she asked.

I opened the cheque and put it on the table. '£79 each.'

Next week the local newspaper informed us that Alice and company had brought the best price at the sale. It was some little consolation for the farmer's wife.

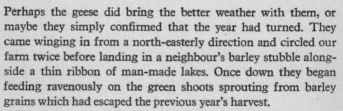 4 Wild geese and goslings

Perhaps the geese did bring the better weather with them, or maybe they simply confirmed that the year had turned. They came winging in from a north-easterly direction and circled our farm twice before landing in a neighbour's barley stubble alongside a thin ribbon of man-made lakes. Once down they began feeding ravenously on the green shoots sprouting from barley grains which had escaped the previous year's harvest.

There were fourteen of them: big, hard-looking birds with black necks and markings which caused Shirley, who had spotted them through the kitchen window, to consult our 'bird book' and announce they were Canada geese. John, our teenage son, climbed on to the hay in the barn to get a better view, studied them through the binoculars, and agreed.

The thought of roast goose made the kids' digestive juices run. They wanted their big brother to take the shotgun and do a Davy Crockett act, but after the long, hard drag of winter it was nice to see creatures which foretold brighter days. Nor, come to that, was there much chance of John getting close enough to shoot. There was always at least one bright-eyed, long-necked sentinel on watch, ready to sound the alarm.

Where the birds came from, where they were going, we did not know, but there was a sense of purpose about them. They moved down to the lakes as the day wore on to spend the night on the water, safe from nocturnal goose fanciers. Just as the last daylight faded a pair of late arrivals circled, calling and honking. They were answered from the water and, reassured, came in to land.

Next morning, when I took the milk up the lane, they were feeding. But by the time I had finished breakfast, done the most immediate chores, and had time to think about them, they had taken off on the next stage of their journey.

They made something to talk about a couple of days later when John and I walked over to Old Jonathon's place to buy wellingtons. The old man believed, so he assured us, in diversification. Somewhere along the line he had entered the clothing business. The truth was that he liked playing shopkeeper.

His emporium consisted of three wooden sheds in the garden so jam-packed with goods stacked on shelves, heaped in corners, and crammed into any convenient recess, there was hardly room to enter.

'Now,' he said delightedly on learning the reason for our visit, 'let's see what I can sell you.'

He rummaged in one higgled-piggledy pile and came up with a pair of khaki trousers big enough to accommodate a bus. I pointed out that they were six sizes too big, I did not want trousers, and there was a hole in the seat.

'Mice,' he said disgustedly. 'Now why should they eat a pair of trousers?'

The answer was soon forthcoming. Some enterprising female mouse had made a nest and successfully reared her family in that particular pile of clothing.

'Ah well,' he said resignedly, 'I'll try sending them back to the makers if I can remember where they came from.'

He tried, vainly, to sell us a variety of things including sunhats, anoraks, battledress tops, flannel shirts, waterproofs and ex-RAF greatcoats.

'Well, I dunno, you'm a fussy couple,' he said finally in disgust. 'Don't you want anything but wellingtons?'

We did not and after fighting off a half-dozen suggestions for alternatives, including fancy American cowboy boots, we made our choice. Plain working wellingtons!

'If you'm satisfied, I suppose I'd better be,' he said grumpily. 'I'll make a special price for you.'

He led the way to the greenhouse which also served as an office and made a cup of tea. I mentioned the geese and he said, 'Them birds have been coming to Egerton or hereabouts as long as I can remember. You see them go, they'll head south. They'm going somewhere special, that's for certain. Sometimes you'll hear them go over at night. They don't like flying in the dark so they keep calling out to one another to keep in touch.'

Big Billy, his outsize but gentle employee, came in with another visitor, a salesman. The slow-moving bachelor had a hole in the knee of his trousers.

'The old folk used to call them the Devil's Hounds when they heard them at night, Jacky,' he said. 'It's a sobering sound to hear when you'm on a lonely road. It's like Old Nick might jump right on your back for a bit of a lark.'

The other man, who was almost as big as Billy, said, 'I heard about a bloke up in Wales who went poaching and took a shot at some wild geese that were grazing. The whole lot took off, high and away towards the town, none looking as if they'd been hit. But when he gets home everybody's yacketing on about some old woman who's hanging out clothes when a damn great goose falls bang, bolt out of the sky into her cabbages. Sunday dinner from the Almighty, she said it was, and knelt down and prayed. This poor bloke that had shot the thing daren't say one word.'

John and I thought it was funny but Old Jonathon simply nodded. 'Some of them Welsh is terrible poachers. One time I was working in a field along the road when a car stops and a big, red-nosed fellow with a gun leans over the hedge and makes to blow the innards out of a tame little cock pheasant we'd reared so it was like a chicken. He hadn't noticed me. 'What's you doing?' I asked him. 'Nothing,' he says, cool as a cucumber. 'Just taking a few practice sightings.' And he doffs his hat and off he goes.'

'How'd you know he was Welsh?' I asked curiously.

Old Jonathon looked surprised at the question. 'You can always tell. Them Welsh is terrible poachers.'

He turned to the salesman and eyed his girth. 'Now you looks a young fellow that knows a bargain. Would you be interested in a pair of trousers with a bit of a mousehole in the back, if I knocked something off the price?'

Our resident geese – the bullying gander Moses and his subservient wife Martha – made their own contribution to the burgeoning season. For some weeks now the poor old goose had been sitting on a clutch of eggs in a nest made in the front of the hay barn and relieving the monotony by hissing madly at anyone who approached too near.

She had little option because her spouse patrolled the area and clobbered her comprehensively if she appeared to be neglecting her duties. The feathered biddy shrieked and scurried about to try and evade the beatings, but never – much to Shirley's disgust – challenged his male right to punish.

Their previous efforts to start a family had failed; the eggs had been infertile. This time they were more successful. The second Sunday in April three eggs – the other four were addled – hatched and produced three fluffy, yellow goslings. As might have been expected with such parents, one of the young birds fell out of the nest in its early struggles, landed on a ledge below and died. The survival of the other two was little short of a miracle.

When they were two days old Martha decided to take them to the pond. Fortunately we saw the goose convoy set out on the fifty-yard journey; the pompous Moses in the lead, then the two goslings, and Martha in the rear. Well and good until Peter the Jack Russell and Spot the collie ran over to investigate.

The gander hissed and threatened, but then, as he always did, broke and raced for the safety of the water. Poor Martha simply panicked and floundered about blindly screeching although no one was chasing her.

Both goslings chased after the gander. One ended stuck helplessly in some loose wire netting, and the other fell into the water and would, had I not quickly intervened, have been swept into the pond outlet pipe to be spat out into the duck-flighting lakes two fields below. As it was I managed to plonk my wellington into the pipe entrance, grab the gosling and carry it to the safer edge of the pond.

The guilty dogs took off with their tails tucked in when I

shouted. They had simply been curious. It was very different with the cats, the biggest threat to the goslings, until they got used to them. They would stalk the pair with infinite patience, moving closer and closer when the goose parents were occupied elsewhere.

Several times it was only the intervention of some member of the family which saved the newcomers. No running for the felines; when they were discovered, they simply brazened it out. They pretended it had all been a game and came, tails up, to be stroked. But eventually even they accepted the goslings and everyone got used to seeing the ungainly yellow creatures waddling round the farm with their parents or, suddenly transformed into graceful movers, sailing about the pond, usually with their oafish father showing off to try and impress on them what a fine bird he was.

5 Feeding the growing grass

The air was full of change. For weeks we had been plodding along in limbo; now, seemingly overnight, the world shed its winter snakeskin and emerged new and bright and busy. It was as if an invisible pulse had begun to beat, almost imperceptibly at first but with an increasing vigour. The land had come to life.

The streams which marked most of Egerton's boundaries ran brown with earth and foamed impatiently at obstacles which blocked their way. Hedges thickened with new budding growth; the verges of the lane were studded with spikes of cow-parsley, willow-herb and cuckoo's pencil; and, most important of all, the new grass came through.

No matter what the calendars might say, every true countryman knows that spring comes in with the grass. In the city the end of winter meant putting away scarves, forgetting gloves and changing to a lighter raincoat. Here it meant ploughing, sowing and freedom for the cattle after nearly five months' imprisonment in their sheds and yards.

Our friends urged caution.

'Don't you go shouting out too soon,' our neighbour Willem said. 'I've knowed snow come in April so thick it was shoulder high. Two weeks before we could get out and about.'

His, and everyone else's efforts were wasted: we were bubbling like the brooks.

Apart from the promise of better weather and easier going, the new grass meant saving on expensive concentrates fed to the cattle, especially the dairy cows. Normally the milkers were 'paid' four pounds of dairy nuts for every gallon after the first which they were supposed to produce from their maintenance feed. But when they were on new grass these concentrates were not needed. Nor would the hay which had fed them throughout their incarceration be required, although there would need to be a transitional period to allow their four stomachs to convert to the new diet. Personally what I most looked forward to was the time when they could stay out overnight, because that would mean the end of dirty udders and muck-encrusted teats.

One evening John, who always hurried home from school to help, and I were busy with the milking when Ellis the Cowman, the quiet little man who taught me which bits of a cow to pull and which to leave alone, walked in. We had no illusions; the attraction for him was the cows, not us. Having been much involved in their purchase, he tended to feel responsible for their well-being. On this occasion he looked them over carefully, prodded and pushed at the incalf ones and pronounced himself reasonably satisfied with our stewardship.

For him our bony-hipped herd were very superior creatures. 'You know, Jacky,' he said seriously, 'it's daft to think that people is better than cows. You read the papers, it's nothing but robbing and killing. You ever hear of a cow being mixed up in anything like that?'

Offhand I could recall no reports of such happenings.

'There,' he said triumphantly, the case proved, at least to his satisfaction. He hung his cloth cap on a nail protruding from the wall and took over the milking.

When it was finished, Ellis came into the kitchen for a glass of Shirley's homemade wine: elderberry – purple, pleasant and very potent. He was a favourite of hers. She liked to hear him talk. He had spent much of his working life building up a herd of pedigree Friesians only for them to be sold and dispersed when his employer retired. For him it had been a traumatic experience.

'I left the land and got a job in a factory out near Birmingham,' he said and shuddered. 'I don't know how men can stick it, day in, day out, all the noise, machines, shouting. I'll tell you, I kept looking out of the window and all I could see was my cows. That was when I missed them most of all. In the end I went to the gaffer and asked for my cards. He thought I was mad. I found some bits of work and then God smiled and we got our place.' The small farm he and Thomas worked was two miles further along the main road.

Our conversation was feed costs and the low price given for milk. He said, 'You should get working on the grass, Jacky. You got fertilizer, start spinning it out, the sooner the better, meet the grass, bring it on.'

For once, I was prepared. It was a smug feeling. There was a ton of nitro chalk fertilizer in plastic sacks, each holding one hundredweight, stored in the garage. An old spinner which had cost £12.50 at a farm sale the previous autumn was housed in a lean-to. It resembled a giant metal ice-cream cone set in a tubular steel frame. Someone, at some time, had painted it a sickly green and someone else had brightened it up with spirals and blobs of bright colours, reds, golds and cowslip yellow, probably using up odd bits of paint. The end result was a candy-stripe nightmare guaranteed to raise local eyebrows almost to disappearing level.

The fertilizer, in granular form, was loaded in at the wide end of the cone and fed out at the pointed end via a control plate operated by two cords pulled by the driver. The granules dropped on to a spinning plate which broadcast them over the grass. The rate at which the fertilizer was allowed through the perforated control plate could be varied and the speed of the tractor determined how fast the spinning plate revolved and how far the grains were flung.

The morning after his visit being dry and bright, the ground being firm, and having no reason for delaying the operation, I trundled out the colourful machine and coupled it to the back of the tractor as per the instruction booklet.

My first problem was lifting the plastic bags high enough to load the machine. They were slippery and there was little to grasp, and while our rustic friends might consider lifting one-hundredweight sacks child's play, I had not yet reached that stage. However, after a struggle I succeeded in balancing the sacks on the edge of the cone and then slashed them open with a knife.

Operating the spinner was simple enough but a couple of practice runs showed up a serious snag. The spinner plate was rusted and paper-thin, eaten away by fertilizer, and some of the ridges which channelled the granules had vanished altogether. A replacement was needed and that involved visiting George Wheatley, whose workshop was situated some four miles from Egerton. A telephone call confirmed that he held the necessary parts and so, without more ado, I set out.

Driving a tractor along country roads and lanes is a splendid activity on a nice day – and this was a very pleasant morning. The countryside was clean and new, green tinted with spring. Everyone seemed to be out working, taking advantage of the weather, beginning the spring routine. Some of them recognized me or, more likely, the tractor since they had an eye for such things, and waved, others turned to look curiously, wondering who I might be and what my business was. It seemed a very few minutes before I turned into George's compound.

The concreted yard was littered with tractors, some modern, some definitely vintage; others had been cannibalized and would never run again. The workshop was a big prefabricated building. Inside the walls were lined with metal racks stacked with spares, tools and accessories; lifting-chains fitted with pulleys and hooks hung down from heavy crossbeams; a welding kit, metal rods, oxygen bottles and smoke-marked torch had been stacked in one corner; a tractor stripped down to the frame stood over one service pit, and a battered old Austin saloon which was having a new exhaust fitted straddled the other.

George himself was an easy-going man in his thirties, tousle-haired, oily green overalls, and grease-blackened hands. He was talking to three men when I backed the tractor through the open doorway into the workshop. One of them, the tallest, a thin, greying man, eyed the colourful spinner and exclaimed: 'What the hell is that? Something out of a circus?'

'It was like that when I bought it,' I explained.

Whatever they had been discussing, George seemed happy to escape. We had had previous dealings. 'What is it then?' he asked.

I indicated the trouble and he scraped about with a screwdriver and finally pushed it right through the offending plate. 'No mending that,' he agreed and promptly bent the plate, tore away a sizeable chunk and held it up for the trio to see. 'Look at that.' They did, and turned to me with accusing eyes.

'It was like that when I bought it,' I explained again.

They looked at one another.

'I'm busy,' George said indicating the trio. 'Can you leave it?'

'He ought to have had fertilizer out afore now.' The speaker was a short, tubby man wearing an expensive tweed sports jacket over a collarless shirt, and a knitted woollen hat complete with a pompom.

George rummaged among the boxes in a rack and produced the required part.

'I'll have a go at fixing it myself, if I can borrow some tools,' I said.

The trio – the third man was a quiet, older man – nodded approval and George said, 'Help yourself.'

They went back to their discussions which seemed to get rather heated and I collected a couple of spanners, studied the machine which suddenly looked extremely complicated, and went to work.

First interruption came from George who glanced over, frowned, and said, 'That's no way to tackle it.' He took over the spanner.

The tall one disagreed with him. 'He was right, it just needs a bit of heat to free the nut.'

George ignored him and worked on.

The older man, who had a slight squint in one eye, said,

'You'll break it going on like that.'

'There's always a first time ...'

'If I could have a go,' I tried, but was ignored. The four of them abandoned their own affairs and clustered round the spinner, heaving and pushing, knocking and tugging, criticizing each other and, at times, sounding on the verge of fisticuffs.

In no time at all the floor was covered with bits and pieces. The tall man pulled the new plate away from George, only to have it snatched back again. 'Give it to me,' the tubby one said triumphantly and fitted it into place. An argument arose as to whether he had done so correctly. It seemed to be settled by majority vote which did not include me.

George's wife came in with a cup of coffee for him and was ignored. She was a tall girl in jeans, with fair hair restrained by a headscarf. The two of us stood looking at the busy quartet.

'You'd better drink this,' she said resignedly and gave me the coffee. It was very welcome. By the time I'd finished it, everything was about done. There were no bits left on the floor.

George wiped his hands on a wad of cotton waste and handed it to the others. He noticed the mug in my hand and said, 'Was that the wife that came in?' I nodded. 'She said for me to drink it.'

'Better not to let it waste,' he agreed.

The trio finished their final inspection of the spinner and the tallest climbed on the tractor and started it to see that everything was working. 'That's all right then,' he said, getting off. 'You wants to get back out there, this weather might go.'

The others nodded agreement.

'What about payment?' I asked George.

'The plate and odds and ends came to about five pounds,' he said. 'Then there's the fitting ...'

'Fitting!' the trio exploded as one. 'Who fitted what?'

'I helped,' he protested. 'Say five fifty total? Leave it, I'll send a bill.'

The others were satisfied. They watched critically as I climbed on the tractor to leave. As I started the engine, I heard the woolly-hatted one say plaintively, 'I've forgotten what we was talking about.'

Back home it was pleasant chugging along about five miles an hour, up and down the twelve-acre field which undulated down to the smaller of the two streams which marked Egerton's boundaries. The new plate was very effective. The fertilizer fanned out behind in a generous arc, pattering down on the grass like wedding rice. It was necessary to keep an eye open to avoid too much overlapping, but this was not difficult.

My frequent trips back to the garage for fresh fertilizer attracted Shirley's attention and she helped me swing up the sacks. Even with breaks for lunch and several mugs of coffee and tea, the work was finished before John and the kids returned from school. All that remained to be done was sit back and wait for the grass to grow.

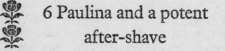

6 Paulina and a potent after-shave

In suburbia there was a little man who almost haunted the horses of the local riding school. Whenever they trotted by he appeared with a little shovel and bucket and collected the precious droppings. Presumably he grew roses.

Egerton would have been a seventh heaven for him. Our predecessors had bequeathed us a veritable mountain of muck. It was rich brown-to-black aromatic stuff guaranteed to stimulate the most reluctant of plants. We were made aware of its presence whenever the wind blew from the west.

But if our townee noses wrinkled, the locals, especially Thomas, Ellis the Cowman's son-in-law, positively drooled. He ran his fingers through his bush of wild hair, stirred a corner of the mound with his wellington and said, 'There's near enough to cover most of the farm. Better than all that expensive bag muck. It's natural, it lasts longer and it won't wash away with the rain.'

When it was disturbed it certainly smelled potent.

The upshot of our fortune was my first experience of muck-spreading. There was some discussion among our friends about whether early spring was the best time to spread, with the new grass beginning to appear. The general opinion was that although it might, initially, blanket the new fine growth, the muck would soon get 'taken in'. We decided to go ahead.

My first problem, as ever, was machinery. Not having a muck-spreader meant having to hire one. After some haggling and much interference from our friends in The Forge, a local contractor, who also farmed, agreed to let me have one for a week at the exceptionally favourable price of five pounds – cash in hand.

This generous concession, which came after an initial charge of twenty pounds had been mentioned, was immediately greeted with scepticism by the same characters who had harried the poor man into reducing his price.

'There's no profit in that,' Howard declared scornfully. 'You might as well let him have it for nothing. What kind of business-man are you anyway?'

The other man sighed. 'There's no pleasing some folk, Jacky. I dunna know whether it's best to have him on your own side, or speaking for the other bloke.'

The machine, when I collected it at the weekend with our trac-tor, was a barrel-shaped rotary spreader capable of taking two or three tons of manure at a time. A central shaft running the length of the barrel was powered by the towing tractor and as it turned iron chains attached to it flailed the muck into small pieces and sent it flying out over the ground. The setting of the curved lid could be varied to determine the angle at which the threshed manure was thrown out and thus control the area covered.

Thomas, who was working for an all-in £1.20 an hour, arrived on the Monday evening driving a tractor fitted with a fore-end loader – a mechanical shovel – to scoop up the manure and dump it into the spreader. The following morning, after breakfast, when the milking and other chores had been done, he appeared with a second tractor towing his own spreader which was the same type as the hired one.

Muck-spreading is not an occupation for the fastidious. It was certainly not something I had ever aspired to, but the grass had to be fed. As for Thomas, the whiffs and pongs went unnoticed; he loved just about anything and everything mechanical and hopped about excitedly, loading and then switching tractors for the spreading.

'Keep an eye on the wind,' he told me.

'Why?'

'You'll see,' he said, showing white teeth in a grin and chugged off.

He was working at the opposite side of the field, covering the ground in a hairpin pattern. It looked straightforward enough, so I drove to my ordained starting point, revved up the tractor, operated the lever which controlled the power-take-off shaft driving the threshing chains and began.

The wind was in my face, the spreader threw the pulverized manure high into the air behind me, the noise was deafening but not unpleasant. Behind me, as I progressed, the machine left a wide swathe of nutritious manure, just the thing to set every blade of grass slavering.

Thomas had emptied his load and was back at the dung heap. He waved and shouted but his words were lost in the noise. I waved back to let him know things were going well.

It was when I turned at the far end of the field to begin the run back that I realized what all the gesticulations were about. The wind was behind me. While the heavier pieces of muck continued to be flung out over the field, the smaller, finer particles came floating gently down: on my back, on my neck, in my hair. It was no use panicking, so I accelerated and kept going but by the time I arrived at the far hedge I could have nourished a fair crop of grass.

My helper, Thomas, was waiting, almost choking with laughter. 'Didn't you see me waving?' he chortled, knowing damn well that I could not have understood what was meant. There was no doubt in my mind that he had been aware of what would happen. 'Always go into the wind or spread across it so that the wind carries the stuff away from you.'

I spat something unthinkable out of my mouth and brushed my hair with my fingers.

'Everybody's got to pay for experience,' he said, totally unrepentant. 'Anyhow, they say it's good for the skin. Some rich women make mud pies out of it and slap it all over their faces.'

There was only one possible retort and I made it.

By lunchtime I was getting quite expert, even if one or two minor miscalculations did result in me being briefly enveloped in clouds of the pungent particles. When Shirley called us in for the midday meal, I shed my sweater and washed under the outside tap. There was no point in cleaning up properly before we had finished for the day.

The complication came in the late afternoon, by which time, sweater back on, I was in a breathtaking state. My wife arrived with the news that one of her special friends, due to spend a brief spell with us, had arrived a day early and was waiting at the railway station, seven miles away. The car was in the garage being repaired, Shirley did not drive Old Lil, the diesel van, so would I collect the visitor, Paulina?

'What, now? Like this?'

No time to quibble about appearance, I was informed, and shoved, with considerable encouragement from Thomas, into the van and sent on my way. 'Don't worry, she'll understand.'

On arrival at the station, I found our guest sitting composedly on a bench reading a magazine. The fashionable coat, nylons and high-heeled shoes were more fitted for a garden party than a long weekend on an impoverished farm.

'You're here sooner than I expected,' she said.

Her nose wrinkled but she did not comment on my appearance. There was one case; I picked it up.

'Been working,' I explained, indicating the muck-flecked sweater.

'Really?' she said, her eyes widening. 'Not regional costume?'

We reached the van and I opened the door for her. 'The car is in dock,' I told her.

She nodded. 'I hardly thought this would be first choice.'

'You get a better view from a van though,' I tried, conscious that the seats were filthy. 'See over the hedges, that sort of thing.'

'You've changed since I saw you last,' she said sweetly. 'There's a certain something about you. Is it the after-shave?'

I was not impressed with her humour. 'Muck-spreading; my first attempt. Marvellous stuff for putting on the grass.'

'Oh,' she said. 'You put some on the grass as well.'

It was time to change the subject. 'You're older than I remember,' I said gallantly. 'Have you been ill?'

'I'll-mannered country lout,' she said, and laughed.

My treacherous, two-faced wife had no hesitation about which party to support when we reached Egerton. She was impeccably turned out in freshly laundered jeans and sweater and had also, obviously, managed to snatch a bath while I was away collecting the visitor.

'He's like this all the time,' she said, after the customary exchange of greetings. The kids, who had returned from school, supported her by holding their noses.

'You poor thing,' our guest said, and they went inside leaving me alone.

Thomas had finished work and gone. He would return the following morning. I put away our tractor and sneaked inside, keeping out of sight, for a quick bath.

When I came down again, the two women were working in the kitchen, preparing the evening meal. Paulina had changed her dress for flared green corduroys and an embroidered smock.

'Ah,' she said, looking surprised and offering a cool cheek when I joined them. 'I didn't smell you come in.'

In spite of our guest's presence and comments, Thomas and I carried on spreading. In five working days we manured over half the farm's seventy-five acres. Two weeks later the growing grass had all but covered the signs of our work, but the benefits continued throughout the year. No matter how hard the fields were grazed, the grass always came back, green, thick, stronger than ever.

The farming wheel had begun to turn; slowly at first but build-ing up pace imperceptibly until events and dates came rushing towards us. It was so with the grass. Every day we trudged up to peer over the gate into the Twelve-Acre to see whether it was ready for us. Suddenly it was.

Towards the end of April it was several inches high. Just right for cows who need something to wrap their tongues around and draw into their mouths. 'A nice little bite', was how the locals would put it.

But anxious as we were to turn out the cows, the new growth was too precious to permit our four-footed providers to graze it *ad lib*. If they were allowed to free range, they would wander about choosing the most succulent feed, trampling more than they ate.

Strip grazing was the answer, so our electric fence, which had been stored away the previous year, was brought out, the battery recharged, and set up to limit the herd to an acceptable area.

It was a Sunday morning when they went out for the first time. The day was dry and crisp; the air so clean and fresh it tasted on the tongue. Our first requirement was to convince the cows that their imprisonment was over. After milking they had ambled back to their yard to get at the hay spread out in the long wall racks. Even when they were on the grass, they would need to be fed hay for some time to allow their digestive systems to convert gradually to the new rich feed.

When we went into the yard to bring them out, they were suspicious of our intentions at first. But then Gaffer, the boss cow, got the message and ambled through the door and the others began to follow. Last to go, as always, was Whitey, the big old cow who was reluctant to exchange her place at the hay racks for what might simply be a Sunday stroll.

They had been penned since the previous November, although on odd days, when the ground was frozen hard enough not to cut up and spoil, we would let them out for a few hours' exercise.

But today was the real thing. They soon sensed it and began to hurry, making for the open gate to the Twelve-Acre which had been closed to them throughout the winter.

Through they went at the trot, pausing to snatch a few quick mouthfuls before following one another in a swaying, bovine conga line along the electric fence and round the confining hedges. Even Whitey forgot her bad back and hips enough to find something a bit faster than her usual crawl, but there was no exploratory jog round for her. Once in the field she put down her big head and set about eating the stuff before someone took it away.

By the time we collected them for the evening milking, they had cleaned up the strip as efficiently as vacuum cleaners. They lay together under the west hedge, sheltered from the strengthening breeze, happy and content, like tired children at the end of a school outing.

Our bonus from the grass was a marked increase in the milk yield. We soon began putting an extra ten-gallon churn on the stand. The snag was that as output, ours and every one else's increased, the price we received for it went down. When I complained about the injustice of this to Jock, the little Scot who drove the Milk Marketing Board's collecting lorry, he grinned and said, 'Now you're beginning to talk like a real farmer. You want summer weather and winter prices all the year round.'

It was all a matter of supply and demand. Some dairy farmers favour spring calving so that cows benefit from the new grass when they are at their highest yield. Another school believes in autumn calving so that, although they have to be artificially fed, cows produce most when the milk brings its highest price. Ellis the Cowman, our guru in these matters, favoured the spring grass theory. Our own feelings were that as our herd increased – the rate was governed by the availability of finance – we would try and arrange it half spring, half autumn and thus ensure a more constant income. The guaranteed monthly cheque of city days was something we both remembered with fond nostalgia. But we were managing and the outlook was improving.

This optimistic mood brought me a reproof when I walked

40

into The Forge a week or so later and found Old Jonathon holding court with a collection of his cronies.

'How's you getting on down there?' he asked.

'Not too bad,' I told him. 'Doing quite well really.'

The gravity of the situation caused him to put his flat cap on and he sat there and studied me like an outraged judge before speaking. 'By God, Jacky,' he said at last, 'that's a dangerous thing to say when any damned outsider might hear. Don't you go round opening your mouth to such words. Just remember, now you'm a farmer, you've got to learn to moan.'

His bench mates nodded their agreement. There was nothing for me to do except beg the court's indulgence and buy them half-pints of bitter beer.

It was the night of my unfortunate lapse into optimism that a worried Howard phoned after we had gone to bed.

'Bring young John and lend us a hand,' he said. 'I've got trouble here with a cow calving. Can you come?'

No question of refusal. He had done far too much for us even to consider such a thing. I roused John and we dressed hurriedly.

The time was a quarter past eleven. It was cold. Above us the moon was like a silver penny sliding among thin cloud. In the field above the house the owls hunted over the grass, screeching to startle mice or voles into movement which would reveal their presence. Something squeaked in the stockyard, probably some unfortunate rodent caught in the open by one of the cats. My son, taller than me now, pulled his coat tighter round him and shivered.

'Howard's arranged this badly. No sense of timing.' He climbed into the family car, the 1800, and we set off.

Our friend was waiting anxiously for us. He looked tired as he ran a hand through his grizzled hair and said, 'I'm sorry to fetch you out. I've got a calf stuck, coming backside first, I wants you and John to pull him for me.'

It was a good enough reason. A good bull calf was making £40–£50, maybe more in the auction ring.

We followed him into a strawed pen where a young cow, Hereford-Aberdeen Angus by the look of her, was lying chained to a

41

heavy post in a cubicle. She looked suspiciously at us and scrambled to her feet.

'First calver,' Howard explained. 'Too big for her to bring and he's coming arse first.'

'How d'you know?' John asked. He had begun attending evening classes organized by the Agricultural Advisory Service.

'The tail's there,' Howard told him. 'Put your hand in and feel if you like.'

John was prepared to take his word for it.

'How're you going to do it?' I asked.

'I can reach the back feet,' he explained. 'If I can get a couple of bits of rope on them, you and John can pull him while I guide. You do as I say like.'

We promised to do exactly that and shed our outer coats.

The cow did not protest when he washed his hands and went to work. He brought out the feet far enough to tie on the short ropes. A lot of natural lubricant had been lost, so a soap solution was substituted.

When we began to pull, the calf's back legs, tail and rump were soon in view with Howard trying to guide the emerging animal. When most of the calf up to the rib cage was free, he motioned for us to put more weight into it. It was imperative now to get the calf clear as quickly as possible. One of the dangers of a breech birth like this was that the animal's stomach and entrails could be forced forward to press against heart and lungs, sometimes fatally. We followed his signals, timing our pull with the cow's own efforts. There was a brief hold-up with the shoulders and head but then it was over and the newborn lay on the straw. It was a brown bull calf.

Howard picked it up by the forelegs and shook it to get the stomach back into its correct position. There was no obvious sign of life.

'He's gone,' our friend said, sounding, for once, rather helpless.

John came to the rescue. 'Help me get him over the barrier,' he said and grabbed the calf.

We slung the little creature over the low wooden wall which divided the pens as he demonstrated.

'Now, if I can remember correctly,' he said and proceeded to raise and lower the calf by its forelegs, causing the stomach to slide forward and compress the lungs and then withdraw again in a pump action which created a vacuum and drew in air.

It worked. There was a gasped intake of breath and the calf's lungs expanded. Its whole body shuddered and suddenly the creature began to breathe. We placed him for the young cow to clean up.

'Well, I'm damned,' Howard said, shaking his head. 'A lifetime in farming and never saw that done before. Live and learn, they say, and it's true.'

'Anything else you want to know?' John asked him jauntily.

Howard laughed as we all stood watching the cow and calf. 'Don't think I wouldn't ask.'

When all was well we went into the kitchen to have a cup of tea. Dilys, Howard's neat wife, in quilted dressing-gown and warm bedroom slippers, poured it for us. She listened as her relieved husband told about the calf's birth.

'Never seen it done afore,' he said.

She winked at John behind Howard's back. 'That just goes to show there's some things even you don't know.'

Half an hour later we were back home. I crawled into bed beside Shirley who stirred and asked, 'Is it all right?'

'A brown bull calf,' I said and switched off the light. It was half past one, the alarm would go off at five o'clock.

The very next day we had two calves ourselves. No trouble with either. The cows had been segregated in two calving pens. The first birth came about lunchtime; a fine black bull calf. The second calving was about eight o'clock in the evening. It was a sturdy black and white heifer.

Our system now was well established and tried. We guided the newcomers to the cow's teats for their first feeds of colostrum. This is the first milk the cow produces after calving. It contains antibodies, which protect the calf against harmful bacteria, vitamins, and it also has a strong laxative effect which clears out the newborn's intestines.

After this first feed the calves were taken away and the mothers went back into the herd. For a few days, until the colostrum

cleared and their milk was acceptable to the dairy, the cows were
milked into a special churn and their milk was bottle-fed to their
calves. It might seem harsh but we had found it to be the most
efficient and least painful method of rearing. If the cow and calf
were allowed to remain together too long, both moped badly
when the inevitable parting came. This way they both got over it
very quickly.

The truth was that the calf, valuable as it was, was still only a
by-product. The object from our point of view, if not the cow's,
was the production of milk.

8 Cabbage plants and sowing

Everything and everyone was buzzing. The sap began running
up again in the trees. Our friends began to shrug off winter and
look to the earth. Machines and implements were brought out
and prepared for work. Men walked their fields, dogs at heel,
assessing whether the land was dry enough and firm enough for a
start to be made.

Our five-acre field near the farmhouse had been ploughed in
November and left for frost and snow to break up the soil. Time
now to work it down into the fine tilth needed to sow barley seed.

That necessitated borrowing a set of discs. From whom else
but Howard? Everyone borrowed them, so why not us? I rang the
man himself.

'You'm welcome if you can find out who's got 'um,' he said.
'It'll cost you a beer, mind you. And if you do find them, bring
them back here after. Likely I'll want them myself in a day or so.'

There was only one man to ask where the discs were; Griff at
The Forge, our local Mr Fixit.

'Why ah, young Medlicott that farms down by the brook; he's
got them. Give him a ring to make sure. I'd imagine he's finished
with them now.'

They were there. I brought out the tractor and set off quickly before anyone else could get to them.

Medlicott was a moonfaced, overweight man in his early thirties. He blinked at me from behind National Health glasses.

'They'm over here,' he said and led the way into an adjoining field.

'You look as if you'd lost a pound and found a penny,' I said. Not an original saying; Old Jonathon often trotted it out.

'Damned sheep,' he explained. 'Look.'

The previous week he had planted the seven-acre field with cabbages. The idea was to take the end product to Birmingham Market and sell them at a profit.

'There's money to be made, I'm sure,' he said. 'Townee folk'll pay anything for fresh greens when they'm short.'

I remembered Shirley's comments on the high cost of vegetables in our city days and kept my peace.

'What do you think of that?' he asked with a sweep of his arm.

All that was left of his enterprise were rows of leafless stalk stubs. The plants had been bitten off about an inch from the ground.

'Damned sheep got into the field and finished the lot,' he said.

'Your sheep?'

'There was some of Geoff Bradley's,' he said. 'But most was mine. Pushed their way right through the hedge.'

'What are you going to do?'

He shrugged. 'Start again, I suppose, when my heart comes back. No good waiting for someone else to do something.'

I wished him better luck.

This was not the first time I had borrowed the discs. They attracted the usual ungrateful remarks.

'You take it easy on the roads or they'll drop to pieces.'

'Hasn't anyone else round here got a better set?' I asked.

Medlicott pinched his nose with thumb and forefinger and grinned.

'No one that's daft enough to lend them.'

'Or generous enough?'

'Don't you go saying that or he'll start getting ideas, but that's about it,' he agreed.

The discs were awkward-looking things but could be fitted with wheels to move them on the road. Medlicott helped get things set and closed the gate after me.

'Watch out for traffic.'

I left him leaning on the gate, cursing woolly coated thieves.

An hour later I was working in the Five-Acre. The wintered furrows crumbled under the tractor wheels and the plate-like, knife-edged discs churned and sliced the brown earth, bringing order to the uneven surface. First, lengthways up the field and back, then across the furrows, and finally lengthways again.

Behind the discs came the usual army of birds searching for grubs and insects. Plumed plovers – 'peewits' locally because of their call; cocky, confident wagtails, awkward on the clods, long tailed, like dapper city gents in black and white suiting; heavy beaked crows; and hordes of goose-stepping, speckled starlings which turned into sea-green jewels when the sun caught them.

They were welcome to what they could find. Their company was more than payment for anything they might take.

In the middle of one run something on the ground caught my eye. When I stopped and climbed off to investigate, it proved to be a horseshoe. Before me other men had worked this same earth, only they had followed behind a pair of tall, trampling horses, shires no doubt, going through the same procedures to prepare the land for planting. I tucked the iron shoe into the tool-box behind the tractor seat and that evening nailed it to the dairy door, remembering to keep it upright so that the luck would not spill out.

The evening milking and chores interrupted the work. Fortunately the weather continued and I completed the discing the following day and then ran over the field with the spike harrows to finish it. The end result was, to my eyes, very satisfying. One of the nicest things about farming is the sense of achievement that goes with so many jobs. Sometimes, contemplating an ailing bank balance, I thought it was the only reward for all our labours.

Two days later, on a Saturday, hawk-nosed Price from the top of our lane turned up, jacketless, of course, in spite of the chill wind, plus his red-haired, giant-of-a-man, younger brother, and sowed the seed for us. It never failed to fascinate me how he drove the seed-drill, covering the area in a series of seemingly haphazard twists and whirls, but, in fact, following an established pattern which ensured that not one square foot was missed.

Last year we had sown into turf, ploughing in the grass, allowing it to rot and fertilize the growing seed. This time fertilizer went in with the seed.

'That's her then,' Price said when it was finished. It was almost a major speech from him.

'What next?' I asked.

'Nothing else to do but sit down and wait,' he said with a sudden smile lightening up the long, saturnine face beneath the thick, dark hair. 'Be off then,' he said and left.

John, who had been following the drill with our own tractor, towing a chain harrow to make sure the seeds were covered, drove up. His fair hair was tangled from the breeze, his khaki shirt open at the neck. He looked hard and healthy.

'What was Price saying?'

'Not much. Just that he'd finished.'

He pulled a face. 'Unlike him to waste words. Anyone could see it was finished.'

I conceded the point. 'It must be the better weather getting him down.'

Two weeks later the barley came through and the whole field shimmered in the morning air like a silken sheet. By autumn it would be golden, hanging its head like a tired child, ready for the harvest. As Price said, all we had to do was wait.

When, that same evening, I returned the discs to Howard, he was busy with barbed wire, staples and stakes mending fences.

'You found them then.'

I told him about Medlicott's cabbages.

'A lot of hard work wasted. It's happened to me. One year some cattle broke into this place, through this very hedge, and played hell with an acre of cow cabbage that was supposed to be winter feed. You get some old sheep, especially old ewes that's been running on the hill, and they'll damn near smash through a stone wall.'

He examined the discs carefully and decided they were good for a few more seasons. No point in spending money on unnecessary tack.

'They all goes on about them, but they always comes back to borrow them,' he said with a wry smile crinkling his weathered features.

We walked round his sheds to look at his stock. The breech birth calf John had saved was thriving, but in another pen a red-coated, white-faced bull calf was thin and wasted from the diarrhoea which kills so many calves. It got up from the straw and came towards us on shaky, uncertain legs.

'Are you getting much trouble with the scours down there?' he asked, giving his fingers to be sucked. 'Sometimes I thinks it's in the walls here.'

'Shirley does most with the calves and seems to cope very well these days, but we will lose one now and again although nothing like as bad as in the first months.'

Now I looked more closely, I could see that he was drawn and tired.

'Up all night with this little'un, wasn't I?' he said. 'Not much to be done. I don't think he'll get through but you can't let'um die without a struggle.'

There was not much to say to that.

We went into the kitchen for a cup of tea made by Dilys, his plump little wife. Her face was shining from a recent bath and her hair was in pink plastic rollers.

'Going out tonight, to a British Legion do,' she explained in her lilting happy voice.

'You ought to join,' Howard said. 'You'd be very welcome.'

'It's the time,' I told them. 'There never seems time for anything but work.'

'Think of all the money you'm making,' Howard teased.

'Money?' I said, falling into the trap. 'What money?'

They both laughed. 'That's it, don't you let on. We all know you'm making a fortune down there.'

A few days later I met him at the market. He was selling some barren ewes.

'How's that sick calf doing?'

He shook his head. 'Died a couple of nights after you saw him. Nothing I could do. I paid out £35 of good money to buy him; it all went with him.'

 ## 9 A bit of muck for luck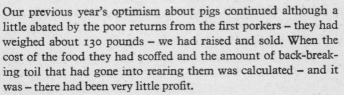

Our previous year's optimism about pigs continued although a little abated by the poor returns from the first porkers – they had weighed about 130 pounds – we had raised and sold. When the cost of the food they had scoffed and the amount of back-breaking toil that had gone into rearing them was calculated – and it was – there had been very little profit.

However, pigs offered a relatively quick cash return and our financial state was such that not even the smallest profit could be overlooked. Our creditors, the local merchants and the bank manager, were very tolerant but with the end of the financial year every post seemed to bring a fresh batch of bills.

Our stock now included four breeding sows – two of them born and raised by us on Egerton – and four gilts, the name given to sows which have not been to the boar. Much more immediately important, there were twenty-nine piglets ready for market. This time we were going to sell at the weaner stage – eight or nine weeks old – and let someone else have the cost of bringing them on to porker or heavier weights.

So, one April morning, Shirley and I loaded the twenty biggest piglets into Old Lil and set off for market. It was not quite as easy as it sounds. The auctioning of pigs began very early, well before the other livestock, so entries had to be in about 9.30 a.m. and that, because the milking and other morning chores had to be done first, meant a mad scramble at the farm end.

Fortunately the weaners weighed about thirty pounds and so could be picked up and carried. We did just that, although it was a case of 'first catch your piglet'. I chased them round the pen, grabbed a back leg, and lugged them to the van while Shirley, in best sweater and tartan skirt, prettied up for a foray among the town shops, with a list of wants as long as her arm and raring to go, held open doors, cheered, gave verbal encouragement and counted the captured. In short, there was pandemonium! The piglets shrieked and squealed all the way to the van but then, once inside, began happily nosing among the thick layers of straw covering the floor.

It was a pleasant journey although Shirley niggled constantly about a half bale of straw we were taking along. Her back rested against it and she was afraid of getting straw in her hair. There was really nowhere else for it to go, so I considered her very unreasonable.

'Then you have it behind you,' she snapped.

This was patently unacceptable as I was driving and Old Lil was never a vehicle one could leave to her own devices. She needed constant attention. But when I pointed this out to my wife, she sniffed and said, 'Perhaps I'd be better off on four wheels.'

This apart, nothing went wrong. Old Lil plip-plopped along at her usual gait, a staid thirty-five miles an hour, refusing to be hurried but covering the ground steadily. We arrived in good time and backed the van into the reception area where a clever arrangement of swinging gates made it easy to offload and channel our piglets into two sales pens indicated by a pleasant, round-faced character in a brown overall who also noted down the details for the auctioneer.

The disputed straw was divided between the two pens, our pigs began to root hopefully in it and before many minutes had passed were attracting attention from potential buyers. One of them, a tall, white-haired man in corduroys and worn sports jacket, asked, with a suspicion of Welsh in his voice, 'Is there any luck on them?'

'Naturally,' I assured him nonchalantly although it had never crossed my mind. 'There's twenty shillings on the lot.'

A second man, tubby and short, ruddy faced and untidy clothes, listened to the exchange and asked, 'That go for me too?'

'It goes with the pigs.'

There was obviously some rancour between the pair. The short one grinned and nodded at the taller man who glowered at him.

This 'luck' was a strange thing. After transactions buyers often expected luck from sellers. It could run into pounds, but more often it was in the form of silver coins. The correct ritual – and at its best it was that – was apparently to spit on a coin, rub it dry against your sleeve or on the seat of your trousers, and hand it over with good grace. There was an element in the practice which reached far back into the past. It was simply inviting misfortune not to offer a fellow a bit of luck.

The main auction was already in progress. It was held in a huge covered market across the road from where we had brought our weaners. There was time to take a quick look.

There were hundreds of pigs. The butchers, many from nearby Midlands towns, moved in a white-coated group bidding quietly against one another, filling their quotas, as the auctioneer with his clerks and helpers moved along the narrow walkway above the tubular steel pens and called bids and took offers.

When the pigs were 'knocked down' to a buyer, the caravan moved on and two market labourers in PVC leggings and rubber boots climbed into the pens with hand implements and punched a hole as big as a new one-penny piece in each animal's ear. The idea was to make sure that no one could claim a second selling subsidy on them.

The pigs squealed and tried to dodge but the men were deft and experienced and there was no escape. They dealt with a pen, usually eight or more pigs, in quick time and moved to the next. There was surprisingly little gore and the pigs seemed not much concerned after the initial 'bite'.

Like all such markets, it might, superficially, appear complete confusion, but it was, in fact, a well-organized machine. Even as the auctioneer continued along, the first batches of pigs he had sold were being ushered along the aisles and loaded into double-decker lorries to be taken to the abattoirs. They would end up as bacon or pork.

Weaners like ours, breeding sows, with or without litters, and the puffed, balloon-fat pigs intended for the process market – pork pies etc. – were housed in a smaller building but the pens and the basic layout were the same. Butchers would be interested in the super-weight pigs – they could weigh 600 pounds or more – but the men after breeding stock and weaners were a different crowd. Mostly they were farmers who grew their own feed barley and were intent on converting it into pork. One or two were men with contracts with local authorities, schools or hospitals, which enabled them to obtain waste food and feed it as swill to their pigs.

Shirley was both fascinated and repelled by the grossly fat 'process pigs' on offer. They made the Egerton sows appear very slim and dainty indeed. Mostly they were animals whose breeding days had finished so that they were no longer of use. Some were so fat they found it tiring to stand and preferred to sit or lie.

One old Large White sow sat on her backside like an outsize dog, her great swollen jowls hanging down, eyes hardly visible in the rolls of fat, and stared jaundicedly at the people inspecting her. When a young butcher prodded her with a cane walking-stick, she grunted but could not be bothered to make the effort to move out of his reach.

But huge though she was, the prize for the biggest animal there must have gone to a monster crossbreed boar. He was enormous; long enough to fill the pen by himself, almost touching back and front barriers at the same time. We did not hear his weight called out but he, undoubtedly, outweighed anything on offer. He had probably got too heavy to be used for breeding. Any sow must have buckled under his weight. It is possible to use a service crate in which the sow stands and which has platforms to take the weight of the boar. This one had probably outgrown even that arrangement.

Most of the sows with litters preferred to ignore inquisitive humans and get on with feeding their families, many of whom could not have been more than two or three weeks old. The piglets looked small and dainty, crowding greedily at the banks of teats offered by their prostrate mother. The sows grunted reassuringly to them, and sometimes, when people went a little too far in their examinations, raised big heads from the concrete to fix the disturbing ones with a 'do you mind' look.

The clanging of a handbell announced the arrival of the auctioneer, a heavily built, elderly gentleman who had some difficulty getting on to the walkway over the pens and needed a stool to do so. But once in position with his entourage, he began selling at a fast rate. His heavy walking stick smacked down repeated as he called out, 'Sold to Mr Andrews', or some other name.

In quick time they had reached the three pens of weaners before ours. The cheapest lot went for £6.40 each. They needed worming, according to what a foxy-faced man told his neighbour. The third pen and the best made a level £7. Not very promising; we had hoped for more than that.

Happily things picked up when the auctioneer reached ours.

'Here's the pick of the market,' he sang out. His clerk pointed me out and he called, half question, half statement, 'Sell the two pens together?'

'As you like,' I said.

'Right, then, here we go. Twenty good strong weaners, wormed and ironed, strong as cats, they'll pick up weight quickly, not waste an ounce of food. What am I bid? Say £7 to begin?'

The tall man came in eagerly. '£6.50.'

'They'm worth more than that, Mr Lewis,' the auctioneer told him. 'Who'll say £6.75?'

The short man would.

The auctioneer grinned. 'I thought you'd be about. Make it straight seven.'

Everyone else stood back and let the pair of them fight it out.

The tall man ended in possession having paid £7.50.

'I made you work for them,' the other told him with a crooked grin and walked off.

The triumphant one looked after him and then told anyone who wanted to listen, 'They'm good pigs. They'm worth every penny.'

I produced a one-pound note from my pocket and offered it.

'Rather have silver,' he said.

Shirley went off to the cafeteria and came back with the necessary change.

He pocketed the coins and then asked, sheepishly, 'You don't have a bit of dry muck from their pens, do you?'

I did not and not even Shirley had anticipated such a demand.

What that was about or what rankled between the tall one and the short man, I never found out.

We left and went to watch the beef cattle being sold before walking to the market office to collect our money – £10 in cash, the rest, less commission, in cheque form – and heading for the nearby shops. Fortunately Shirley's enthusiasm had evaporated. She bought a few essentials, splashed out on a gigantic bottle of green liquid shampoo, and settled for a fish and chip lunch in a café much frequented by farmers and their wives. Flushed with success, we indulged in second cups of strong tea before returning home.

Altogether a successful day. There might not be a fortune in weaners but there certainly seemed more profit and less work than in producing porkers.

A week later I took the remaining nine to market. Alone this time. Shirley did the door opening bit but preferred to stay behind. She was painting the kitchen.

There was no sign of the previous week's buyer or the short man but a slim, well-dressed young farmer paid £7.40 for the batch. I dug in my pocket for the required 'luck' but he grinned and said, 'Buy me a cup of tea instead.'

It proved he was university-trained, managing his family's farm, and more interested in ascertaining that the pigs had been properly dosed and inoculated than taking my silver.

When I got home in plenty of time to enjoy the hare casserole she had prepared, my wife asked, 'How much?'

'£7.40.'

'Hm,' she said slyly, 'not as good as last week. I should have known better than let you go alone.'

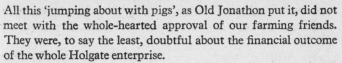
All this 'jumping about with pigs', as Old Jonathon put it, did not meet with the whole-hearted approval of our farming friends. They were, to say the least, doubtful about the financial outcome of the whole Holgate enterprise.

'Money going down the drain,' Big Billy, the heavy-weight farm labourer who worked for Old Jonathon, declared. 'The only thing to do with pigs is eat them. Make pets of them and they'll want to sit at your table. If you don't eat them, they'll eat you.'

'There's a few pennies here and there in them,' our neighbour Willem said. 'Not many, but a few here and there.'

'Backache and bother,' Billy said unrelenting.

The discussion, as usual, was in the public bar of The Forge. It stemmed from our intention to buy a boar. This was necessary because Howard had disposed of the huge animal he had kept. It had gone to a relative who was a part-owner or some such thing. The news was a serious blow to our plans.

Our decision was also hastened by Old Lil, the van, suffering from loose doors. We used her often to get the churns up the lane to the stand for collection by the milk lorry. The snag was that as a full churn weighed about 120 pounds and my own weight had dropped from near twelve stone to about ten-and-a-half, a full churn was a fair proportion of my body weight.

So I loaded the churns into the van by hoicking them up with my knee. They went in with a satisfying thump but, un-fortunately, this had caused the floor to sag a little just where the rod which secured the double doors fitted into a receiving hole. Result: the doors could be shaken open if someone or something was determined enough.

Dorfie, our sociable sow, was determined enough to persist and opportunistic enough to spot the weakness.

This was brought home to me with the departure of Howard's boar. Another farmer whose place was about three miles from Egerton had a boar we could use for a fee. So when Dorfie came on heat, I loaded her into Old Lil with the usual bribe of pignuts, slammed the doors behind her, turned the handle, and set out.

The rutted, stony surface of our lane helped jar the rod loose. The doors opened just a crack. It was enough. Here was a weakness. Our porky friend was not the animal to miss such a thing.

A gesticulating road worker gave me the first indication that something was amiss. The sow's head was protruding from the flapping doors. When I pulled in to the side and stopped, she jumped out. Happily there was no traffic.

The gent who had given me the warning came up and helped, although he was somewhat apprehensive about meddling with such a big animal. Her grunts of protest when I slapped her rear particularly alarmed him. But we coerced her into turning around and climbing back into the van. No one could have been more surprised or relieved than me. I closed the doors and tied the handles together with a bit of rope and set off, hopeful that with the smoother, tarmac road they would stay shut.

Not so. Less than half a mile further on the same thing happened again. She forced the doors open despite the rope and jumped out as the van slowed. Nor would she get back in this time. It was like trying to turn a train. She started to forage in the ditch, so I parked the van on the verge, grabbed a broken stake lying by the roadside, gave up all ideas of getting her to the boar, and set out to walk her home.

She was quite happy to go in that direction away from the van. Nor did I have any compunction about making up her mind with the aid of a *whap* now and again. I was, to put it mildly, rather upset.

Before we had gone far, her feet, unaccustomed to hard surfaces, were sore. She limped along like a fat lady in shoes two sizes too small. I kept her moving with some hefty whacks on her rump.

The last remnants of my luck disappeared. Matthew, Old Jonathon's brother, pulled up in a dilapidated old car he had acquired in a deal. His broad, open face was creased with laughter.

'Taking the pig for a walk, eh, Jacky?'

I assured him firmly this was not the case and continued walking. He grinned delightedly and drove along slowly, on the wrong side of the road, keeping pace.

'If you'm going to take her out often, best fit her with a collar and lead.'

I told him, forcibly, to go away. It had no effect.

We passed the road worker who looked astonished but said nothing. As we drew level with The Forge, Matthew sounded his horn. I had hoped to get past unnoticed. Instead the sound brought Griff, the bushy-eyebrowed publican, plus two or three customers, out to see what was happening.

'Nice to see animals being well looked after,' Griff told me unctuously.

'There's folk that puts them in sties and forgets that pigs like to see a bit of the world. I'm glad you ain't one of them.'

One of the men behind him asked, 'Is he the bloke that came from London to farm down at Egerton?'

'He is indeed,' Griff informed him. 'Them townfolk knows how to treat animals right.'

'He must have more free time than me, if he can take pigs out walking,' the man said.

Griff laughed and shouted after me – I had not stopped to banter. 'I'll ring your Missus and tell her to put the kettle on as you'm coming home with a friend, Jacky.'

He did just that and Shirley walked up the lane to meet me and help. One look at my face had her shrieking with laughter. 'They think you've been taking her out for an afternoon outing.'

They didn't, of course; they knew exactly what had happened. It was something I'd have to live down.

By the time she reached her sty Dorfie Pig was tired and wincing every time her trotters touched the ground. I gave her one last hearty wallop, bolted the door behind her, and set off in the car with Shirley driving to retrieve the van.

On the way back we stopped at The Forge for a consolation drink. Matthew was still there, leaning on the walking stick he carried to ease his arthritic back. I resisted an impulse to kick it from underneath him.

'Put the piggy away now?' he asked, gesturing to the grinning Griff to get us drinks.

'Nice to see people caring for animals,' our host said. 'Does a pig the power of good to get out and meet new people, see the countryside.'

Shirley chuckled and handed me a beer before I could explode.

After the farce with Dorfie Pig, we had indeed to think seriously about getting a boar of our own. One of the main advantages of keeping a male animal, apart from convenience, was being able to 'catch' sows immediately they came on heat and get them in pig. The episode with the van doors meant having to wait, and feed our sore-footed sow seven pounds of meal a day for three weeks before she would be ready for the boar again.

So back we went to read our well-thumbed textbooks. According to the experts the costs of keeping a boar could be justified if there were eight sows. Well, with the gilts about ready, we had the required complement.

The pros and cons of the matter were much argued by our friends and unpaid advisers.

'Turn 'em into bacon, they'm about the right size,' Billy advised when he came visiting and saw our four gilts.

It was a thought, but we had motherhood plans for the quartet of bright-eyed animals.

The subject was being aired in The Forge one evening when Aaron, the fat, jovial character who farmed high up on the mountain, came puffing in. It was a chilly night but he wore only a shabby blue serge suit with the jacket unbuttoned to show an open-necked shirt and the tangled black hair on his chest.

'There you are, Howard,' he said on seeing his stocky, aggressive friend. 'I've been looking for you. Your Missus said you'd be here and likely to buy me a beer or two. That's a fine woman that knows how hard it is for us up there on the hill.'

'She said nothing of the kind,' Howard sparked, knowing he was being joshed but unable to resist the bait. 'We all know you've got money rusting in that sock under the bed.'

Aaron shook his head sadly so that his chins trembled. 'You'm a man with harsh words, Howard, but I know you've got a good heart.'

'Buy your own beer,' his friend interrupted fiercely.

The fat man sighed and dug his hand deep into his trouser pocket. 'Well then,' he said cunningly, 'If you ain't going to buy me one, can I get one for you?'

It was the *coup de grâce*. Howard swore and stood up. 'All right, you crook. I was going to get some anyway.'

'You gets more generous every day,' Aaron said humbly, hiding a grin, and promptly sitting in the chair the ex-sergeant had vacated by the fire.

These exchanges were quite in keeping with the pair's friendship. They had been going on at one another for years. What rankled with Howard most was the fact that Aaron's farm was high enough above sea level to qualify for hill farming subsidies whereas his own was not. It was a useful arrow in the other's quiver and one he never hesitated to use.

Everyone was pleased to see the fat man. Like most of them he loved reminiscing. 'When we was kids somebody give my brother a little runt pig to rear. It went everywhere with him. In and out of the house like a dog. Only as he got bigger my mother, God bless her, got to shutting the door against him. That pig never could understand why the dog and the cats could go back and forth but not him. So he'd stand up on his back legs and look in through the window. It gave visitors, specially ladies, a shock to see a pig's nose pressed against the glass and him looking in to see what was happening.'

'Was that a boar?' I asked.

'No, no,' he said. 'My old man cut him when he was no bigger than a tadpole. No, we used to walk our old sow down the mountain to Neville Cadd's place. He'd a good boar. Leastways, the first couple of times we walked her down, all of a mile and a half. After that, when the urge come on her, off she'd go by herself with us running along behind.'

'What happened to the pig?' I asked.

'We ate him, of course,' Aaron said, looking surprised.

'Didn't you mind him being a pet?'

'Well, we was at school when the poor soul was done,' he said.

59

'It was all over by the time we come home. My brother was a bit juggled because it was his pig.'

'Your Samuel?' Howard asked, intrigued. 'What happened?'

'Oh, you know,' Aaron said, wiping the back of his hand across his mouth after a long pull at the beer. 'The old man gave him a bit of a lathering ... and he come round to it. Running around up there as kids, we was always starving. We ate a horse one time.'

That bald statement provoked visible shock among everyone in the public bar even beyond our little group.

'Go on,' Matthew said. 'Eat a horse? You didn't?'

'Did too,' Aaron said composedly. 'Big pony ... belonged to old Lewis that lived near the chapel. He fell into the small quarry and broke a leg and the men had to finish him. It seemed a bit of a waste to leave a big thing like that to the crows, so they skinned him, cut him up and we ate him. Tasted very nice too. They eats them in France all the time, y'know. Frogs and snails as well.'

'No wonder you'm such a strange bugger, it's the way you've been brought up,' Howard said handing him an empty glass. 'See if you can find your way to the bar. It might be difficult because I can never remember you buying beer.' A dozen pairs of eyes studied the horse-eater carefully when he stood up. Horses were ridden in that part of the world, not digested.

'Pigs is all right as pets,' Matthew said. 'But you've got to keep a close eye on a boar. Some years ago I took a sow down to Gaffer Carter's place in the van. Going down this lane, I passed Gaffer. "The boar's in the open at the bottom of the yard," he says. "Put your sow in with him." When I gets into the yard the boar's loose. I get out of the van and go round the back to let out the sow and he takes one look and comes straight after me, mouth open and roaring.

'There's a trailer just by. I jumped on that and he rages round and round threatening blue murder. Then he smelled the sow and starts trying to get at her, biting at the tyres and anything he could get hold of. It must have been near half an hour before he wanders off a bit and I sneak down and open the doors. Back he comes but the sow is out and he starts on her. I'd jumped into the van and closed the doors behind me. I'm still there when Gaffer comes back. By then the boar's worked off all his steam. "Savage? Him?" Gaffer says laughing. "He wouldn't hurt a fly." "No, but he'd damn sure have hurt me if I hadn't reached the trailer," I says.'

'I knew that boar,' Howard said. 'He got good pigs.'

'He did get good pigs,' Matthew agreed. 'But he wanted watching.'

'Not all boars is vicious,' Griff laughed after looking at my expression. 'You should have met our Old Hubert, Jacky. Me and Geoff Bradley down the road had half shares in him. I'd save up all the lees and slops in the pub – chuck them in a bucket – and we'd feed it to him mixed with a bit of ground barley. He loved it. One sight of the bucket and he'd go mad. If he was running with sows, and he usually was, he'd drive them away from the trough and finish the lot. He was a proper old soak. His legs would just buckle when he'd had a skinful and down he'd go, drunk as a lord. Trouble was that although he might fancy a sow when he was loaded, they was safe enough, he couldn't perform because he'd had too much. And next morning! You could all but see the hangover. In the end we had to ration him and make sure the sows got a share.'

'Who's got him now?' I asked.

'No one, he got sick and died. Quite suddenly. It was his liver or something, I think.'

'Cirrhosis?'

'Something like that, the vet said. Big pity because he was a nice old boy.'

 11 Enter Percy Pig

The outcome of all the discussion was Percy Pig. Early one Saturday morning John and I climbed into Old Lil and set off to visit a breeder advertising pedigree Landrace for sale. It meant a round journey of about fifty miles but we were in no hurry, the countryside was fresh and green, we had plenty of time.

The farm proved to be a model establishment. It was a father-son operation with the latter, a square-framed, university-trained young man in his mid-twenties, in charge of the pigs. No nonsense about his approach to the job. He had us paddling around in a shallow bath filled with disinfectant before being admitted to the piggery. No one was going to import disease if he had any say in the matter.

Their operation was aimed at producing pigs at bacon weight – about 200 pounds – and we were shown round and duly admired the stock before coming to the subject which had brought us there.

'These are grown enough to breed from,' he said, indicating a pen of healthy-looking gilts.

But we had our full complement of sows and gilts for Egerton's buildings and had come for a boar.

'There's one ready for use; I'll run him out for you,' he said.

Percy – the family named him after the usual conference – was eight months old, frisky after being penned, and exhilarated with being allowed out. He bounded into the little penned square and kicked up his back legs with the sheer joy of being in the open air. His ears flopped forward and threatened to cover his eyes and he frequently tossed his head to see better.

'He's a good-natured animal,' the young man said. 'Never had a hand or stick laid on him, so he's easy to handle. If you take him, you could use him right away, although he'll grow for a few months yet.'

More for John than for me, the young breeder discussed points in his physical make-up. Our seventeen-year-old held his side of the conversation very well.

As for me, I remembered an old boy saying in The Forge, 'A good pig ought to have the shoulders of a princess and the backside of a washerwoman.'

Well, Percy was obviously male, but he met those specifications well and, as always, when something special walked into the sale ring, quality showed.

'Shall we settle?' I asked John.

'We're not likely to find anything better,' was his opinion.

The price stated in the advertisement was £40. It represented a hefty investment for us but a boar is half the pig herd so we considered Percy a justified expenditure.

Our host led us into the farmhouse to settle accounts. His sister, an attractive fair-haired girl of sixteen or seventeen summers, made us tea, and his mother, an older version of the girl, brought us slices of fruit cake.

'He's worth every penny,' the young man assured us. 'A boar from the same litter went last week to a 200 sow herd. If there is any trouble, give me a ring and we'll take him back.'

I wrote out a cheque and handed it over.

'You'd better have a bit of luck,' he said unexpectedly and produced a pound note.

Old Jonathon and his cronies would have approved of the young modern's respect for tradition.

'Rather have silver,' I told him, playing my own part.

He grinned and his mother opened a tin tea caddy and counted out the required coins.

'There, that should be about right.'

It was exactly right.

With the receipt we got a boar licence issued by the Minstry of Agriculture. It meant that the animal had been inspected and approved for breeding purposes by a Ministry official. When we returned, via the disinfectant bath, the boar stood quietly while the young man lifted his ear to show the crown and identification number tattooed inside.

Loading proved easy. Percy was an inquisitive creature. He bounded along the aisle between the pens to where the van with open doors waited to receive him, stepped on a straw bale put on the ground and jumped into the vehicle with an elasticity reminiscent of a caterpillar. The doors were shut and fastened and it was all over. A metal plate, drilled to take the securing rod and bolted to the van floor, had, temporarily at least, solved the problem of Old Lil's loose doors.

'He should travel well but might be a little doubtful at first as it's all strange,' the breeder said. 'Take things easy.'

We did just that and, apart from a wrong turn which led us

63

along narrow, overgrown country lanes, fortunately quiet and carless, the return journey was uneventful. Percy rooted among the straw bedding and then, lulled by Old Lil's shimmying, lay down and rested.

Naturally, the family turned out to welcome the new arrival. Shirley was a little apprehensive, and the kids expected something out of Tanglewood Tales, all hair and tusks. They took the precaution of being near a strong pen door, ready to nip inside should the boar prove fierce.

I drove the van into the stockyard and we pulled a metal gate across the entrance to make sure the new boy did not make a bolt for it. Our precautions proved unnecessary. Percy came down from the van with the same fluid motion that had taken him into it, did his fresh air jig, sniffed around the yard, and ended by pushing at a door where a young gilt on heat was being held. I opened it and he trotted in to begin his duties.

No problems about him settling down. After the restrictions of the controlled environment set-up he had known, our pens and, in particular, the pig compound with its soil, grass and clumps of nettles, were an adventure playground. On sunny days he lay stretched out happily with the sows; a sultan in his harem. In the two weeks following his arrival, all the sows and gilts went to him.

In quick time he became a favourite with all the family. He was an innocent, trusting creature, never having been hurt by a person, and we proposed to keep it that way, but he was still a boar and the kids were not allowed to treat him with the same familiarity they showed with most of the stock.

A few days after Percy reached Egerton, Howard and Ellis the Cowman came visiting to see our 'folly'. The latter considered money not spent on milking cows probably to have been wasted but, when the boar was paraded, had to agree that perhaps we 'had not done too badly'.

As for Howard, he studied the animal carefully before delivering judgement. 'That is a real pig,' he said finally. 'As good as I've seen anywhere. A real pig.'

John proudly demonstrated the boar's points. His *pièce de résistance* was to scratch the animal's broad back.

An expression of sheer bliss came over the pig's face and, slowly, his legs buckled until, finally, he rolled over for his tummy to be tickled.

Howard shook his head. 'That old boar of mine would have snapped your hand off.'

A few days later he arrived with a sow in his pick-up van. 'Might as well make use of that playboy of yours.'

John, who received the boar fees as perks for looking after the animal, supervised the operation and pocketed the one-pound note.

'One pound for you, two for anyone else, keep it quiet,' he said.

Our ex-sergeant friend approved. Having no son of his own, he took a great interest in ours.

That was by no means the last pound for John. The news of Percy quickly got around and we soon had a steady flow of customers wishing to make use of the boar's virile services.

The gestation period for pigs is three months, three weeks and three days. There were no hang-ups. Percy was as potent as he was handsome. All our sows farrowed over a seventeen-day period. It was hectic but Egerton was quite well equipped for a herd of this size and we coped. The place was overflowing with piglets. The last litter brought the grand total to eighty-eight. We did not have a pen to spare.

The newcomers were healthy and spry. No need to look beyond them for proof that the boar was, indeed, half the herd. From their tiny, curly tails down to their snouts and the floppy ears that fell over their eyes, each and every one was a miniature replica of Percy.

It was seeing Price's cows out grazing for the first time that made me realize it was May Day. The date was very significant for country folk. Rents were often due then, fairs were held and, like our reticent friend, many locals waited for it before loosing their cattle on the new grass.

'It's the proper day,' they said when asked.

The delay certainly gave the new growth time to thicken and strengthen.

Not for us. We needed all the profit we could get from the land. Our milk yield was mounting steadily, clearly showing the benefit of the fresh feed.

It was a very special day when I was able to put five full churns, fifty gallons, on the stand at the top of the lane. Little Jock, the Milk Marketing Board lorry driver, nodded approvingly. 'I shall soon need another lorry just to collect yours.'

The surge in milk production meant extra work for him. A 'platform' had to be rigged on the vehicle to provide extra accommodation for churns. 'Still, it's better to have work than weather,' he said cheerfully. By which he meant that like all of us, he preferred mild May mornings to the trials of winter.

He was a good-humoured little man, no more than five feet two, but he handled the 120-pound churns with an ease which made my own back-breaking efforts seem very feeble.

His mind was on retirement and he had bought a run down cottage on the west coast of Scotland. Each summer he went there to holiday and to work on modernizing the place.

'Folks is all right down here,' he would say with smiling eyes, 'but they canna speak proper English, they canna make porridge, and above all, they're not Scots . . .' His accent came and went to order.

'We have porridge on Sunday mornings,' Nicholas, who had ridden up the lane in Old Lil with me, told him indignantly.

'No, laddie, you just think you do,' Jock told him gently. 'It's Sassenach pap. In my parents' home, when I was your age, you could stand a spoon upright in the porridge my mother made.'

After the lorry had rattled off, Nicholas and I climbed on to the stand to look over the landscape. The terrain fell steadily away from our high vantage point before climbing up to the mountain.

The whole area was cloaked in heavy morning mist. Peaked roofs of farm buildings appeared to be floating without anything supporting them, the tops of taller trees emerged, here and there the line of hedges on higher ground could be traced, and the steeple of a faraway village church could be made out faintly, like an unfinished charcoal sketch.

But this was only temporary. Two hours later the sun had cleared the mist away. The world was fresh and green, splashed with colour. Bright coltsfoot and dandelion decorated the banks, pink blossom marked where crab apples grew, hedges were laced with honeysuckle.

The swallows had returned, swooping above the stockyard, taking up their old nests in the corners and crannies of buildings. It was nice to see them back. It would have been interesting to know how many had survived the trip to and from Africa.

The better weather certainly cheered Shirley. She came bustling in from a calf-feeding session loaded with blossom from the cherry tree outside the kitchen window. She was very pleased with herself.

'How's that look?' she demanded, arranging the branches in a tall, misshapen blue vase, a relic of the pottery class she had attended in suburban days.

'If you pick the flowers, there'll be no fruit,' I informed her unnecessarily, conscious of sounding pedantic.

The response was a rude gesture. 'Last year the hens got more than we did.'

It was not completely true, but the chickens did, surprisingly, prove to be very enthusiastic cherry eaters, even jumping to reach low-hanging boughs.

The arranged blossom looked beautiful and went well with the farmhouse interior; white painted, uneven walls, and low, heavy beams, but the next morning the carpet was littered with fallen petals.

A few days later, I was chain-harrowing the bottom fields to rip away the dead growth and let the sun and air reach the new grass underneath. I had stopped the tractor and was walking to the house for lunch when the cuckoo called from the big ash tree he was sitting in. The sound echoed clear and bell-like, unmistakable, over the meadows. So he was here again! Parasite he might be, but the cuckoo was always a welcome visitor to our little domain.

There was much to be done but the bright days gave us plenty of energy. Fields had to be allocated and set aside for hay. Our experience of the previous year stood us in good stead. John and I got busy with stakes and barbed wire strengthening the fields' defences against covetous stock. In the main we had the better of the annual battle but the sheep never ceased to cast hungry eyes on the tender, succulent feed and patrol the hedges looking for weak spots.

One Sunday Shirley and I, with the two younger children, left John to cope with the farm and took the road into Wales, heading for Borth and intent on a day at the seaside.

The route climbed up into the mountains where trees were scarce and stunted and isolated greystone farmhouses told of the determination needed to make a living from a harsh land. Everywhere there were small nimble Welsh ewes and their long-tailed lambs.

When we stopped for our packed lunch, a farmer came down the hill behind us with two Border collies working a flock of perhaps 300 sheep and lambs. He did little, content to leave things to his helpers. The dogs worked well together with a grey-muzzled bitch clearly the dominant animal. The younger dog constantly looked towards her to see what needed to be done and then raced off to complement her actions.

'Bitch and pup,' the farmer, a thin, bent-backed Welshman wearing an old overcoat tied by string and worn wellingtons, told us.

'What kind of lambing have you had?' I asked.

He hesitated, reluctant to tempt fate. 'Better than average but there's a long way to go yet. You never can tell these things.'

'No one can see what will happen,' I agreed.

The dogs had taken the flock across the road and moved them on towards the farmhouse.

'I must try and keep up with them,' the man said, smiling, and touched his cap to Shirley. 'Have a nice day by the sea.'

When we got there it rained. The waves were grey and leaden. It was too cold for the kids to paddle but it was still a good day. It made a change from the routine. We found a café and enjoyed platefuls of fish and chips before setting out on the return journey.

John had finished the evening milking and was cleaning up when we arrived. The kids had bought him a small stick of rock. They handed it over, received his thanks, and then, shamelessly, helped him eat it.

The conversation was about sheep again when I went into town for a haircut. The barber was an old, stoop-shouldered man who had no truck with modern trends and styles. He had spent most of his working life as a shepherd on the mountain that over-looked Egerton.

'I'd a flock of 500 to look after in them days,' he said in his quiet, rather squeaky voice as he worked. 'Three dogs to help me and no one else. Save at shearing. Then the wife would come along and lend a hand and the kids. Packing, that sort of thing. But it was hard on the back. All right when you'm young but not when you'm grown and fixed. I've known a back so bad I couldn't lace my own shoes ... And it's all hours and little pay. But they weren't bad times. Our kids were young. I think the war spoiled it all, things have never been the same since. The kids grew up and went. They'm either in the towns or overseas. My elder boy is in Australia. I've never even seen my grandchildren. The wife started getting poorly, rheumaticky, so I chucked it all up, picked up the scissors like.

'Now I've got this place, renting it and living above. The wife's happy enough but, to be honest, there's times I miss the hills and the sheep. Some days, when I'm off, I get on the bus and go and walk round where I used to work. Just walk round. Our old house is in ruins now and there doesn't seem half the sheep. No one to look after them, I suppose. I haven't done it lately. Perhaps now the better weather's coming . . .'

An old man waiting, although whether as customer or friend I did not know, said, 'In them days no one was in a hurry. There was time to look round and see what was going on behind. Now it's all telly and motor cars . . .'

I made noises of agreement and paid over forty pence. Looking in the mirror, I could see that he had lost none of his shearing skill. Very little of my thinning hair had escaped him.

The flowering of the may transformed the hedgerows. From our bedroom window it looked as if the fields were enclosed by banks of snow. Everywhere one looked the scene was the same.

The hawthorn played an important role in country-lore. Thus Shirley and I met Willem in the lane and found him shocked at the sight of the may blossom she was carrying.

'Don't you go taking that indoors,' he warned. 'Take that inside, you'll take bad luck in with it.'

'Why?' I asked curiously.

'Because . . . well, it's so, everyone knows it,' he said.

We decided not to risk calamity, thanked him, and dumped the stuff.

Not even our oldest friends could explain just why may blossom should carry such a threat, but none of them doubted that it would be madness to take it into the house.

The little thorn tree, which was common in local hedges, came into the picture again when one of the cows limped into the collecting yard looking very sorry for herself. First thoughts were that she had picked up a nail but an examination of the sore foot soon showed otherwise. The foot was swollen and tender between the clees and bad-smelling pus provided evidence even we could recognize. She had foul of foot.

A quick call to the vet and a description of the symptoms found him in agreement. The complication was that the overworked man was about to start on his rounds, had a very full itinerary, and would not be coming to within four miles of us. However, it was agreed that he would leave a loaded syringe for us to collect and use. It would be concealed behind a stone in a cavity in an old stone wall behind a certain rural telephone box. We had made similar arrangements in the past.

Shirley went along to collect it and arrived to find an elderly man finishing a telephone conversation. His wife was waiting in their car. Both of them were astonished when she retrieved the syringe. It must have looked like an illegal drug delivery. She was still chuckling when she arrived home.

We had kept the cow in the collecting yard. It took only a few minutes to put her into a stall and inject the antibiotic into her rump as per instructions. By the following evening she was walking naturally again.

The vet's prescription was effective but some of the older locals had another way of treating 'foul'.

'First you must watch where the cow puts the bad foot,' Aaron from up the mountain said. 'Then take a knife and cut out that patch of turf. Hunt about until you finds a hawthorn bush and throw up that turf so that it hangs in the branches. As the tuft dies and shrivels, so will the foul go.'

The vet snorted angrily when I asked him about it. 'Witchcraft, like them pushing whole eggs down calves' throats to cure scours. No basis at all in medicine.'

'But does it work?'

'It appears to,' he conceded reluctantly. 'What really happens is that the infection works itself out and disappears. The drier the weather, the quicker the turf shrivels. It's the same with foul. The drier the weather, the quicker it goes. There's a link.'

Some time, he assured me, he would sit down and write a book about these so-called natural cures and show them for what they really were.

In the pub that same evening, Old Jonathon listened to the vet's explanation but said doubtfully, 'P'raps that is it. He could be right. Try it for yourself and see. But remember it has to be a hawthorn.'

'Why can't it be any other tree?'

Several of the characters present looked quickly at me as if I were half-witted. 'The hawthorn is the may tree, Jacky. Don't you know that?' Everyone seemed to consider that adequate explanation.

13 The cattle trade collapses

A tall, stubble-chinned man with a hessian sack tied about his shoulders to make a rough cape was holding forth on the state of the market when I walked into The Forge this evening. It had, he informed anyone who cared to listen, collapsed and the so-and-so politicians were to blame. Give them cheap meat and they couldn't care less about the farmer.

Mine host, Griff, in shirt sleeves with a neat waistcoat, was lending half an ear to the talker while bringing his books up to date.

'Alec here's just been saying that the Government has ruined us all,' he said straight-faced, nodding towards the tall man and closing his ledger to serve me.

'It's true. The French trade's gone. The price of cattle 'as sunk through the floor,' the caped one said.

Having delivered this cheering news, the visitor finished his drink, bid everyone 'Goodnight' and left. There was a roar as his lorry pulled away from the car park.

'He does a bit of hauling, a bit of trading, bit of everything,' Griff said to my unspoken question. 'Something in what he says though. Exactly what we don't need with The Forge sale coming next week.'

The little auction across the road from the pub was a barometer to local life. For generations it had served the needs of the immediate vicinity and the holdings set high on the mountain which overlooked the scene. When stock trotted into the ring, as often as not they carried the hopes of friends of ours.

Local support was vital if such markets were to survive the competition of the sales held in neighbouring towns. Once they had been protected by distance, but the advent of the cattle lorry had changed all that. There was a general approval when I announced our intention to enter six yearling heifers, all raised at Egerton, in the next sale. Brave words perhaps, but the tall man's statement cast a shadow. John and I had been cosseting the bunch to make certain they were at their best when the time came. It was discouraging to learn that our efforts might go unrewarded.

Naturally with our family the trader's pessimism was not sufficient; there had to be complications. They arrived when the kids came galloping down the lane, red-faced and excited, to break the news that they had entered Shirley for another sale – on the same day. This time it was the school's bring and buy. They regarded participation as a great honour for the whole family.

Their mother had different feelings. She was shattered! There were barely enough hours in the day to get through her existing chores without taking on anything extra.

'You'll be in charge of the toy stall,' Vicky informed her happily. 'We're going to look through ours and find something for you to sell.'

It was highly unlikely that any sane person would pay money for the rubbish littered about their bedrooms.

The first impulse of both John and myself was to laugh, but the sight of Shirley's stricken face stifled the inclination.

'The sale is a week on Saturday,' she wailed. 'What am I going to do? What is there to sell?'

A few minutes on the telephone brought some relief. She was needed to fill a vacancy; the previous occupant was producing her umpteenth baby. A young farmer's wife who lived on the far side of the village would also be on the stall. Even better, they had already accumulated a considerable quantity of material and had the promise of much more.

There was no clash of times. The headmistress was a middle-aged spinster who had devoted her life to the school and was far too experienced to make that elementary mistake. The Forge sale was in the morning; the school 'do' was at 3.30 p.m.

Like the auction, the school was an important element in local life. It had about forty pupils and a staff of two: the other half of the staff being a pert, pretty twenty-two-year-old. There could be no question of Shirley withholding her services.

Naturally, from that moment on The Forge sale was relegated to second place. Our economic survival might be at stake, but what was that to raising money for a school outing? The phone hardly seemed to stop ringing; the lane was alive with cars, coming and going; the house was continually filled with efficient country women who ignored the requests of mere men seeking cups of tea.

The amount and variety of stuff collected was staggering. Many of the farmhouses had big attics stacked with the débris of past generations. They were goldmines. The offerings piled up in our utility room.

Nick and Vicky had a great time sorting through it. Their problem was how to read all the books and comics before they were taken to the sale. Personally I considered a big spotted Victorian rocking-horse to be the pick of the lot. The 'stall lady' was much taken with a handmade, delicately carved doll's cot which was more a collector's piece than a child's plaything.

The evening prior to the great sale – the school, not The Forge – the whole family loaded everything into Old Lil and escorted it to school. John and I travelled in the van, Shirley and the kids followed in the car.

The first person I saw in the playground was Willem, our thickset pessimistic neighbour, all resplendent in a respectable church-going suit. He beckoned me to take one end of a heavy trestle table he and his wife were carrying and relieve her. She promptly left us to it. 'Ours is cakes and cookery,' he explained. 'It's been a madhouse at our place these last few days.'

'We're doing toys.'

He nodded. 'Better to keep out of the way and let the women get on with it. You got anything entered at The Forge?'

'Six heifers,' I said, stumbling backwards down some steps into the school hall which was a prefab, separate from the main red-brick Victorian building.

Willem was not a man to waste bad news. 'Market's gone. You can't give cattle away . . . so they say.'

We set up the table and stood by helplessly as the ladies got on with the work. Finally I went to Shirley and her stall companion, a plump, red-cheeked woman, and asked if there was any need to stay.

'Oh, you're still here,' she said surprised. 'I thought you'd gone.'

No such luck for Willem. He had to wait until his wife was ready to leave.

'See you tomorrow,' I told him and got out as quickly as possible.

Next morning Egerton was hopping with excitement. It is always advisable, unless you have anything to hide, to get stock into the auction pens early so that potential buyer can have a good look at them. So, about ten o'clock, John and I, plus the kids, set out to walk the bunch up the lane. They looked very well. They were all Hereford-Friesian crosses; Vick and Nick had curry-combed their black and white coats half a dozen times, and a liberal ration of concentrates had given them a healthy sheen.

There was just over a mile to go but it was a doddle. They walked easily up the green-banked lane, along the short stretch of main road, and into the auction place. Friends helped to pen them.

Everyone was there. Old Jonathon, in flat cap and brown overall, and his broad-shouldered brother Matthew, came over.

'What's you seeking for them?' the latter asked, leaning on his ash walking stick. 'You'll not let them go at less than £72, I'll be bound.'

'Well, we could do with the money,' I told him.

Both brothers frowned. 'Never sell a thing just because you needs the money, Jacky. Sell it when the price is right. If you wants money, steal it, or go to the bank, they'll always advance against stock.'

John had gone along to the office, a small wooden shed, to book in the cattle. He came back carrying a pot of paste, a flat piece of board for applying it, and six round labels bearing the number '11' to be stuck on the heifers' rumps.

'They'm good cattle,' Old Jonathon persisted. 'Don't you let them go daft.'

My son interceded to reassure him. 'I'll see he behaves, leave it to me.'

Our friend nodded, not completely satisfied. What was worrying everyone were reports of depressed prices. No market functions in isolation. The professional dealers who 'set the bottom' at auctions are always aware of what happens elsewhere and cannot afford to go against the general trend. They much prefer a buoyant market with a good trade; giving the seller a fair price, allowing them to make a reasonable profit.

From the start this morning it was obvious that Mark Boyce, the auctioneer, would find the going sticky. The first few lots went at prices which brought murmurs of dismay and disapproval from the farmers crowding the wooden rails.

By the time our lot was called, the pattern had been set. The bidding opened at £55, which caused Old Jonathon to snort, went up to £62, hung fire, crawled to £66, and died.

'Well?' Boyce asked, looking at me. 'Shall I let them go?'

'No damn fear,' Old Jonathon told him before I could speak. 'Not at that figure. He's selling, not giving them away. They'm going home.'

There was a burst of laughter and Boyce waited.

'Sorry, no sale,' I confirmed.

We were not the only farmers to take stock home that day.

Shirley came out of her kitchen to witness our return. 'Not a good enough price,' I said.

'They'm nothing but crooks and robbers,' Vicky informed her. John laughed. 'Old Jonathon's words.'

The midday meal was rather depressed but everyone had cheered up by the time we set out for the school. Trade there was good. The place seethed with clean-faced, healthy children. They soon emptied the toy stall. The rocking-horse went to a tiny two-year-old girl with golden curls as fine and light as thistledown. Another girl, six years old and in Nick's class, got the cot. Our pair settled for a batch of books – some they had not been able to read – and some battered games. By the time we got away, I had spent nearly three pounds and had only a bottle of Pepsi and a small tin of toffees won in a tombola game to show for it.

The final result was a net profit of £93.40, more than sufficient to cover the cost of the outing to the Welsh coast.

That evening Shirley and I walked up to The Forge. There was a definite air of depression.

'You'd think the sky had fallen in,' Howard said, trying to inject a little spirit. 'Cattle will come good again. It ain't the end of the world.'

'You think I was right to take ours back?'

Matthew stirred his bulk on the fireside seat. 'No doubt at all. Give them a few weeks and put them in again.'

Willem, still in his best suit, was sitting quietly holding a pewter tankard. When Shirley moved out of earshot, he asked, 'What kind of cook is the Missus, Jacky?'

'Very good, why?'

'Just that we've got a great big cake she made. Bought it at the school.'

Everyone laughed.

'There's three big jars of pickles in our kitchen and I can't stand the things,' Howard said, grinning. 'They always give me indigestion but Dilys said they were going cheap.'

'If anyone wants anything eaten up, bring it along to our place,' Old Jonathon said. 'Matthew and me does our own cooking. No womenfolk to spoil us poor souls.'

Howard proved a true prophet. Prices did recover. We marched our six up the lane again three weeks later and this time they were in demand. The final bid was £76 each, which was considered very good. Patience and good friends had brought us an extra £69 on the bunch.

'Just you remember,' Old Jonathon said, transparently happy at our success, 'never sell anything just because you happens to need money.'

Sound advice, only our problem was that we seemed to have self-emptying pockets.

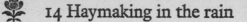

Everyone in the market cafeteria was agreed: something was wrong. June was a growing month; the grass ought to be coming through much quicker. Instead the growth on fields set aside for hay was too sparse to please farmers who must rely on it for winter feed.

'What's more, you look at the colour of it,' Tall Stan, a friend I usually met at sales, said, tucking into a cheese sandwich as thick as a doorstep. 'It's yellow, bleached, like string. There's a need for rain. If grass is to grow properly, it's got to have rain, it's got to have sun. One's no good without the other.'

There was general assent round the table.

'You watch though,' he continued, encouraged by the response. 'The minute we start to cut, the heavens will open.'

His fears came as something of a shock to me. In their happy suburban ignorance the Holgate family had been enjoying the long run of sunny weather. The lambs were growing and fattening, the milk yield was increasing as cows calved and came into production, the pig population, especially the little ones, positively revelled in the warmth. Things were so good I should have known there was a catch.

Aaron, who farmed up the mountain, looked up from behind a mammoth helping of sausage and chips. 'It's building up for something. There'll come a devil of a storm in the next day or two. It's in the air . . .'

His friend Howard set down his teacup with a clatter. 'Listen to him go on. Here's a bloke that doesn't know it's going to rain until his coat gets wet. He's been listening to the BBC again.'

'No radios up there, boy,' Aaron said, pulling a spaniel face. 'Hill farmers can't afford that sort of thing, that's for you rich people.'

It was pure provocation.

'Listen to it,' Howard exploded. 'All them subsidies pouring in. You'm on the pig's back up there and that's no mistake.'

'So, shall we get rain?' I interrupted to separate the pair.

'Too damn much, I fear,' Stan said despondently. 'It'll come down in bucketfuls, flatten everything and run away. What we needs, but what we won't get, is a couple of weeks' steady falls at night and sunshine during the day.'

'Well, whatever we wants, we shall get what comes, and it's sure not to please everyone,' Howard said.

'By God, Howard,' Aaron said sarcastically, 'you'm a chap that knows a thing or two.'

Driving home in Old Lil I could see what Stan had been worried about. The land was baked and parched by the sun. In our city days Shirley would have been in her element, dragging a lounger out on to the patio to sunbathe. Now, here I was worrying because the weather was too good.

My wife was working in the garden when I arrived, using a handfork to put in plants that friends had given her. She stood up and brushed hair from her forehead.

'How was the market?'

'Everybody moaning about the lack of rain. Aaron thinks we're in for a big storm!'

'Feels very like it. The air is full of static.'

'How's the calf?' I asked.

She shook her head. 'No better – worse, if anything.'

For the last two or three weeks we had been nursing a sick calf. It seemed to be a dwarf – at least it never grew discernibly. At six weeks it was little more than its birth size. Shirley and the kids trickled milk down its throat and fussed with it. The vet had given it injections of vitamins and hormones but nothing seemed to work. Most of the time the little animal lay on its straw bedding. If it was raised, it could only totter on trembling legs. It was particularly depressing for Shirley who had most to do with it.

The storm broke about mid-morning the following day. The sky darkened dramatically, turning a slate-grey colour which made the mountain stand out like a cardboard cutout. Puff-pastry clouds floated round the peak like so many balloons held on strings. In the fields the swallows skimmed low over the grass and the cows huddled against the hedges, tails to the strengthening wind, and waited for the onslaught.

It opened with a display of pyrotechnics. Thunder growled and rolled about the mountain, then drifted over Egerton's fields with lightning striking down to earth near enough for me to smell it. There were many stories of animals being killed by lightning and I got very worried about the safety of our precious herd.

I dumped the bale of straw that was intended for the sick calf's pen, and walked into the middle of the field to see what, if anything, could be done. It was a mistake!

The rain came stampeding along the valley like a runaway herd of wild grey horses. I grabbed the straw and bolted for the pen but was soaked before reaching halfway. Raindrops big as grapes exploded on the concrete yard and roofs. The water simply cascaded down from the buildings, overwhelming the guttering.

It was a relief to slam the pen door behind me. The calf was too weak even to raise its head. Fifty minutes later, by the time the storm had blown itself out, it was dead. It simply gave a little sigh and stopped breathing.

Even though it was the first such death on the farm for some time, it came as a blow to Shirley. She got very attached to the calves which responded so eagerly to affection.

'The vet was not hopeful,' I reminded her and went to telephone the Hunt Kennels who would collect the carcass.

'Good grief,' she said on hearing my boots squelching, 'you're half drowned.'

The storm certainly cleared the air and brought some relief to the land but, as our friends had predicted, most of the water ran off the baked earth and was lost. Our pond rose about eighteen inches because the six-inch outlet pipe was unable to cope with the volume of water.

However, the 'flood' brought a bonus for the four geese – the gosling were almost as big as their parents now. A foolish, eight-inch trout forced its way up the outlet pipe and into the drain from the ribbon lakes at the lower, bottom levels of the farm.

The excited geese chased the poor thing all about the pond and made a great outcry. Not able to see the fish because of the muddied water, Shirley and I stood and watched as, one after the other, they plunged their heads under to try and grab the prize.

Naturally it was Moses, the bullying gander, who succeeded. He emerged with the fish flapping helplessly in his bill. The others tried to take it from him – as, indeed, we would have done had it been possible – but he evaded them, threw back his head and swallowed his catch in one great gulp.

'There goes a very tasty breakfast,' Shirley said sadly.

Although it had been over so quickly, the storm had ripped quite sizeable branches off trees in the gulleys which marked the boundaries of Egerton. A few hours' work with a big bow-saw gave us a welcome supply of firewood. There were reports of similar damage from all round the district and a big oak tree was said to have been split asunder by lightning on a farm not very far away.

But it brought a change of weather and was followed by a period of gentler rain which induced growth. Even so the grass crop looked to be well below expectations. The choice soon became whether to cut when the grass was young and tender and likely to make better quality hay, or take a chance, wait a week or two longer, and go for more bulk. In the end, as always, everyone did as the weather dictated.

Nothing looks sadder than wet hay in a field, unless it is the farmer trying to salvage it. There were plenty of both about this year. By the second week in July just about everyone was re-signed to the fact that it would be a bad harvest. The rain that had been so welcome in June persisted, holding back the oper-ations necessary if barns emptied by the demands of winter feed-ing were to be refilled.

As a family we found wet weather depressing. Ours, unfortunately, was not a rich establishment blessed with acres of covered yards and walkways. A few showers of rain and we were squelching about in sloppy mud which worked up the outside and over the tops of wellingtons. The cows brought the slushy stuff into the milking parlour on their feet although the mild rain seemed not to worry them. Worst of all, no matter how carefully we shucked our wellingtons before entering, the mud carried into the house and that meant trouble from Shirley who put great store on cleanliness and was not inclined to accept explanations.

It was a dismal introduction to full-time farming for John who had finished school at the end of June after taking his 'O' levels and was working with me at Egerton. The pair of us slouched around occupying our time with routine jobs, waiting for the weather to change so that we could make a start.

It was all very different from the popular concept of hay-making: happy cider-swigging peasants frolicking around big-wheeled wains, occasionally throwing up a forkful of hay.

We overhauled the equipment. The two interchangeable multi-toothed cutter blades used in the mower were razor sharp and ready for use. The machine itself was oiled and greased. The other essential – the hay turner – came in for similar treatment.

Our friends were in the same predicament. Whenever we met the conversation was the same: the weather. It was cursed and damned as if it were a living, malevolent creature.

Old Jonathon blamed the BBC weather forecasters. 'Them up there in Television Land parading about in their Sunday suits like a lot of Nancies,' he declared contemptuously. 'Why don't they do something? No use them telling us what it's going to be like tomorrow. We needs to know what it's going to be like for the next fortnight.'

Unfair to the forecasters perhaps, but his words summed up the problem. Haymaking requires a considerable stretch of hot, drying sunshine, not just a few pleasant days. The harvest is always a gamble against the weather and the farmer's only advantage is that he starts the game by deciding to begin mowing.

The best quality hay is made from young grass before it flowers, which, in this district, meant cutting about the end of June. Once 'felled', grass must be dried and turned into hay as quickly as possible, preferably without being rained on, if it is to retain its maximum food value.

'It'll lie in the swathe unharmed with a fair amount of water falling on it,' Griff, the benign host at The Forge, said. 'Mind, you can't leave it for ever because the grass will grow up through it, but it'll stay a time. But turn it once and it rains – it'll go bad in front of your eyes.'

Just when we were beginning to think of building an ark, the weather changed. The sun forgave us and began to shine in earn-est. Everything and everyone was transformed. By the third day the BBC abandoned their apologetic manner and forecast a dry spell.

'We all know'd that,' Old Jonathon said.

It was what we needed. The scramble started. John began cut-ting in the Twelve-Acre where we had fenced off about a third of the area because the grass was growing faster than the cows could eat it.

The countryside came alive with the sound of tractors and the rattle of mowing machines. But everyone was still nervous, mis-trusting the weather, studying the sky anxiously, trying to con-vince themselves that they had made the right decision.

In the next few days we cut all our fields even though there were several brief spats of rain. The sun flirted with us and the hay made slowly. Mornings were dull and grey and although they cleared up, there was no real heat in the sun. We worked with our fingers crossed, hoping we were doing the right thing but unable to think of an alternative. When we turned the grass in the Twelve-Acre for the first time, it was almost an act of faith.

Our fears were intensified by several short, sharp bouts of rain but each time the sun fought its way back to the surface again and, eventually, we felt justified in approaching Price, the quietly spoken character who had contracted to do our baling. Even in a good summer haymaking made heavy demands on him because there was always his own farm to run. This year it was much worse because of the uncertain weather; everyone wanted their own work given priority. The pressure showed in the lines creas-ing his long, dark-eyed face.

He walked round, kicking the hay about to check that it had dried right through, screwing it in his hands, smelling it, even biting it, before venturing an opinion. 'This lot can just be baled, the other still needs a day or two.'

That same afternoon he came down the lane driving his big tractor, the squat red baler towed behind and an ungainly bale-sledge bumping along last of all. John was already at work in the Twelve-Acre with our turner, rowing up the hay for the baler to gobble up, two rows at a time, like some insatiable beetle.

Price was never a man to waste time. The baler picked up the hay, compressed it and ejected the neatly tied bales to drop on to the following sledge. When there were seven he tugged a control rope which operated a swing gate and dumped the bales on the grass stubble.

By the time the last bale appeared, the meter was recording 431; not a lot, perhaps, but a bonus because the field had not originally been earmarked for hay.

The next stage after baling was stacking. This farmer's wife was an experienced, if not enthusiastic, stacker. In our first year she had learned the hard way that bales of newly made hay weigh between forty and fifty pounds each. Furthermore they are tied with rough binder twine guaranteed to ruin ladies' hands. She came equipped with stout gardening gloves.

'I just hope your precious cows appreciate what has to be done for them,' she groused as we worked, building stacks of seven bales each. The grouping made possible by the bale sledge saved much walking and carrying.

'What an ungrateful person you are,' I told her. 'Thousands of women pay large sums of money to go to health farms.'

She nearly exploded. 'Health farms! This is more like a forced labour camp!'

In spite of the uncertain conditions we managed to get all our hay baled. The final total, according to the meter on Price's machine, was 2,432 bales – almost a hundred less than the previous year but still very good.

The fifteen-acre field at the bottom of the farm was the last to be baled and we worked until after dark to finish the stacking. Next morning was depressingly grey with drizzling, wetting mist and it stayed that way without a worthwhile break for the next two days.

Andy, a short, stocky Scots engineer friend, arrived from London to help out. His arrival must have inspired the sun and we went through a period of nearly a week without rain, working like madmen to get the crop under cover. Many of the bales would have been thought too damp to lug in a normal year so we spread them out in the bays to dry. The generated heat and the steam made the barn like a Chinese laundry. There was an obvious risk of spontaneous combustion but we were prepared to take it.

Three weeks after beginning cutting, we lugged the last bale, dropped it into place, and promptly headed for The Forge and a celebratory beer. It was a tremendous weight off my mind. Egerton's finances could not have survived a winter if we had needed to buy hay.

Not everyone was as lucky as us. For most small farmers, unless they are blessed with strong sons, a good wife and willing friends, haymaking is a trying time especially if the weather turns against them. Some had hesitated before making a start and had been caught by the returning bad spell. There were many stories of hay turning black and rotting in the fields. Some farmers had simply to wait until the whole sorry mess dried and then set fire to it.

'As bad a season as I've known,' a grey-haired old boy said in The Forge. 'Them of us that's lucky enough to have feed in store ull have to draw on it. Them that ain't got it will need to buy and it'll be a hard price. Maybe next year'll be better, it's certain sure it can't be a great deal worse.'

 ## 15 The season's task – shearing

Every season brings its special tasks. The warmer weather drew the grease up in the sheep's wool and fired the life systems in the big blowflies which buzzed about the flock. It was time to shear the ewes and rid them of their heavy winter fleeces before they ruined them on the brambles or became infested with fly maggot.

It was much easier the second time round because we knew what needed to be done. The Wool Marketing Board had already registered us and supplied three 'sheets' – great voluminous hessian sacks in which to pack the shorn wool. With these came labels and a postcard to be mailed when the wool was ready to be collected.

More important still, we were slotted into the local routine. This was a time when the young men augmented their incomes by contracting out their skills as shearers. There was a great rivalry and banter among them because shearing is a skilled craft and they were proud of their ability. The reigning champion was a small, dark-haired man whom I had seen in action the previous year at a friend's farm. He worked like a machine, using the electric clippers to remove the fleece in one piece, following a pattern of 'cuts' or 'blows' designed to shear the entire animal with the minimum movement. When the flock was finished, it was still possible to identify the ewes he had clipped even though there had been three other men working.

However, he was whispered to be 'unreliable', a bit of a ladies' man, and addicted to the 'bottle'. Informed opinion was that Morris Jones, the tall, thin young man who had sheared our little flock the previous year, would topple him from his pinnacle in the near future.

Normally the shearers worked in pairs, forming larger groups to cope with the bigger flocks which could run into many hundreds. They had to be up and away with the light, working until it was too dark to see and tottering, increasingly tired, into bed in the evenings. But shearing was their share of the wool harvest and they had no intention of losing it.

Our sixty-five ewes represented a couple of hours' easy work for one man, but at 12.5 pence a fleece they added up to what the locals called 'a tidy sum'.

Jones had us on his list of clients and rang to confirm that we wanted him. 'I'll fit you in then and let you know the night afore I come. If the weather's playing up perhaps you can bring them under cover and keep them dry.'

This was exactly what happened. The uncertain weather complicated the shearing just as it complicated haymaking. Wet sheep cannot be sheared and there were several days of foot-stamping as the young men waited for a spell of dry days.

We benefited because, whereas normally we would have expected to come after the large flocks, Jones rang up one morning from a big hill farm to ask if we could have our sheep ready for the following day. That afternoon we ran the flock into the big covered cow yard where the herd had spent the winter months.

The floor of the yard was a 'frozen sea' of straw and manure, dry enough because the cows had been outdoors for over two months, but very uneven. By the next morning the 'billows' had been ironed out by the small, neat hoofs of the flock. It made it easy to see why sheep are so invaluable in fixing or firming agricultural land.

There was a bit of a scramble after the milking but everything was ready when Jones's battered old car appeared at the lane gate. The ewes and lambs together were confined in one half of the collecting yard, restrained by a combination of a ten-foot gate and tubular hurdles.

The other half of the yard had been swept, scrubbed and cleaned to ensure that no bits of straw or foreign matter fouled the wool during packing. Dirty wool brings a lower price. The first big sheet was ready, tied into an improvised frame, waiting to receive the fleeces. The actual shearing would be done on a portable wooden 'floor' left behind by one of our predecessors at Egerton.

All Jones had to do was connect his electric shearing machine to the extension lead hung from the steel beams of the yard to give all-round movement, put on sacking overshoes to provide a better grip on the floor when it got greasy, as it must, and call for the first ewe.

The flock was edgy and nervous but they were closely packed and it was easy enough to catch the first animal, a small-boned Welsh halfbreed, and drag her to the shearing point while her lamb looked anxiously through the gate bars and called to her.

For shearing, the sheep were upended and sat on their rumps. It was always astonishing how easily the locals like Jones handled animals. A sheep that had fought me all the way to the 'floor' would lie supinely against the shearer's legs like a child's plaything while he bent, straight-legged, to his task. When I commented on it, Jones laughed and said, 'Ah well, by the time we'm been shearing a week or so we smells so bad, they thinks we'm one of the flock.'

The clippers chit-chatted merrily, the belly wool came off first and separately, the fleece followed in one piece rather like an unwanted coat. In a matter of minutes the shorn animal, looking rather embarrassed, was released and back in the flock and another had taken her place.

Either John or I packed the fleeces, rolling them up and twisting the tail into a rope to wind round and secure the bundle, tucking the end under itself. Before long the sheet began to fill.

Shirley arrived with coffee and stood and watched for a few minutes, even taking a turn with the broom we used to keep the shearing and packing areas free of bits. But she declined our invitation to take a turn catching or packing, even though I assured her that the grease beginning to coat our hands and forearms was lanolin and said to be good for the skin.

Her suggestion that Jones share the midday meal with us was refused. His job involved too much bending and there would be nothing solid to eat until he had finished that evening. 'Better go a bit hungry than have the cramps,' he explained. In the course of the shearing season he would lose a stone or more.

Two maggot infestations came to light, the first when the clippers stripped away the wool at the base of a sheep's tail and exposed a seething mass. There was the usual distinctive odour of decay.

The second case came to light when shearing showed up a deep but partly healed wound at the back of an elderly ewe's leg. The wriggling white monstrosities were feeding in the wound.

'Dogs,' Jones said after examining the gash. 'Something's been after her. Some damned stray dog by the look of it. She must have shaken him off.'

John sprayed the infected areas on both sheep with blue antiseptic from an aerosol. The colour would make it easy to pick out the two ewes for later checks.

'There's a lot of maggot about,' Jones said. 'I heard about a bloke at Sollars who was down sick for a couple of weeks, no one checked the sheep and he lost five good lambs from the fly, eaten right through into the guts.'

With three of us working, the shearing was finished before midday. The last two sheep John did under our guest's supervision. He proved quite expert and Jones said, 'You ought to come along with me and Ned, my mate, next year perhaps. A little bit of experience and you'd be a useful bloke to have around.'

Then it was over for another year. The last ewe ran thankfully back to the flock. Our shearer took down his tackle and packed it away. We all washed in the hot water from the dairy boiler and went into the kitchen to scrounge tea and settle our account.

I wrote him a cheque for £8.12. He tucked it into his leather wallet and made an entry in a little black pocket book.

'You've got to keep accounts,' he explained. 'Me and Ned pool our earnings and split them down the middle at the end of the season. Fairer that way.'

He left us soon after and headed back up the lane for his next stop – a small-holding run by an old man who had once been a butler in London. Twenty ewes should be waiting for him there.

John and I had not finished with the flock yet. We marked them with our sign, a large red 'E' for Egerton, dosed all of them with a medicine to control gut-worm and other parasites, and then, much to their relief, turned them loose. They streamed down to the bottom fields, obviously happy to be free of our attentions. The sheared ewes had a 'naked' look, but the weather, if moist, was warm and none of them suffered from their fleecing.

The result of the day's work was two sheets bulging with fleeces. We laced them tight, labelled them, and manhandled them into the foodstore to await the collecting lorry. In the evening Shirley and I walked up to The Forge and posted the card in the square pillarbox outside the pub. A week later two cheery characters arrived, lifted the sacks on to their lorry and took the wool away to be graded and priced.

It was October before the post office van came bustling down the lane and its driver handed over the mail and declared, 'Most of them's bills but this one looks interesting.'

He waited while I opened the envelope. The wool cheque had arrived: £57.70.

'Thought it might be that,' he said. 'Everyone seems to be getting them today.'

Not riches, perhaps, but our sheep were primarily meat animals and the wool was only a by-product.

A couple of weeks after the shearing Old Jonathon rang up to tell 'the Missus' that we could walk the sheep round to his place for dipping. Everyone except Shirley came. John and I plus the kids and Spot the sheepdog walked the flock up the lane and along the road, just under two miles, to his farm.

As always he was delighted to have company, and hurried about telling everyone how to do exactly what they were doing. His brother Matthew watched him thoughtfully before saying, 'You'm like a barnyard hen 'uthout her head, Jonathon. Leave things alone and let's get on with the job.'

But the old man was not upset by the criticism. 'You've got to put on a show or they won't think they'm getting their money's worth.'

Theirs was a prosperous farm. They had been working it for the last half-century and had nothing to learn about raising live-stock.

'It gets no easier though,' Matthew said, setting up a diesel-driven portable shearing machine which he proceeeded to use to 'clean up' clinkered muck around some of the sheep's rumps. 'There's more money about than when we started here but folks don't seem much happier for it.'

Their employee, Big Billy, had come along to help. John took up a wooden 'paddle' and positioned himself about halfway along the rectangular concrete bath which was filled with an oily-looking pesticide guaranteed to rid the sheep of scab, maggot, lice and ticks. The kids sat on the wooden railings to watch; Old Jonathon, resplendent in too-big PVC leggings and a straw hat, was Master of Ceremonies.

When he gave the word, Billy and I started catching and put-ting the sheep into the dip. The previous year I had almost gone in myself with the first few sheep, but this time I was more wary.

'Like this,' Billy reminded me with a big grin and caught a big, bony Clun Forest ewe, turned her neatly and slid her quietly into the brown brew. 'Back end first . . .'

I followed his example but cheated, selecting the smaller ewes and the fat lambs, leaving him to handle the bigger animals.

Before long there was a steady procession of sheep swimming through the dip, ducked under by John's paddle if they had managed to avoid immersion in the first plunge. At the far end they scrambled up a sloping concrete ramp. The excess solution drained off them and ran back into the dip.

Old Jonathon's eyes twinkled. 'You've learned a thing or two since you was here last, Jacky.'

'Enough to let Billy take the big ones.'

'He's strong enough and daft enough to dip bullocks if they'd got to go through,' Matthew said, stopping his machine. 'Ain't you, Billy?'

The big man looked thoughtfully at him. 'I'm waiting for the day Jonathon says you'm to go through.'

Around the halfway stage, Old Jonathon called a halt and went off accompanied by the kids. They reappeared with cans of Coca Cola and bars of chocolate and he carried a big jar of his homemade cider. The drink had a certain local reputation.

'Guaranteed to knock flies off the wall at five yards distance,' Big Billy said as he swigged a hornful. 'It tastes a bit better than the dip but gives you more of a headache.'

'Here, here,' Old Jonathon protested, 'it ain't that bad . . .'

In fact the cider had a pleasant, dry flavour: very more-ish. But I had learned my lesson about handling farm cider, as well as handling sheep; two generous tastes and I declined. There was a lot more work to get through before the day was out.

The break, or perhaps it was the cider, helped. The remaining animals were soon put through and the last to go, a plump, blocky lamb, clambered out dripping and ran baaing to find its ewe.

'That's it then,' Old Jonathon said. 'Do you want to put the kids through?'

But there was no sign of Vicky or Nick. They had returned home, taking a short-cut across the fields, eating their chocolate bars as they went.

All that was left was to check the numbers dipped and see if we agreed. The brothers and Billy ran the flock from one pen into another via a narrow passageway.

'One hundred and thirty-five?'

We had no dispute.

We went down to Old Jonathon's greenhouse which also doubled as his office and study to complete our business. I made out a cheque to a round four pounds and handed it over.

'Now you wants to get them into market and cash them in,' he advised. 'Don't go hanging on. Get them there early, afore the price drops.'

He showed us his kitchen garden and cut two big cabbages for Shirley. 'Give her these with my respects,' he said and added a pot plant, an African violet, for good measure.

We made our farewells and departed. The collie kept the sheep moving along and took them down the lane to Egerton at a pace which left me well behind. Shirley looked out from her kitchen window as the flock, still brown and damp from the dip, streamed past the house and through the waiting gate into the eight-acre field.

'You smell of sheep dip,' she said, wrinkling her nose when I presented Old Jonathon's gifts.

She was right. The stuff had a distinct, pungent tang. I tasted a spot on my forearm. 'The cider is definitely preferable,' I told her. She put a finger against her forehead and made a screwing motion.

 16 A woolly lawn-mower

Our suburban friends, the Robbies, rang up and asked if they could spend the following Saturday, two days away, with us. They were more than welcome, but for some feminine reason the thought of their coming threw Shirley all of a heap.

She rushed round the place in a frenzy, scraping and polishing, rearranging furniture, even taking down the curtains in the end bedroom where they were to sleep and washing them although they were almost new.

'What's the panic?' I asked. 'Dorothy is probably your oldest friend.'

'That's just it,' she said enigmatically.

I regretted asking the question: it seemed to make matters worse.

Fortunately the state of the lawn escaped her notice until it was too late. It was a nice lawn, big and square, but it had been neglected for years and was lumpy and uneven. Some of the grass had stems like bamboo.

Cutting it with our light petrol mower was a nightmare only excelled by trying to cut it with the hand-mower. Our more muscular visitors sometimes tried to repay our hospitality by tackling the job but always gave up and settled for easier, pleasanter chores, like mucking out calf pens or cleaning pigsties.

It must have been when replacing the curtains that Shirley spotted the state of things. She came down the stairs so quickly, I thought she'd seen a ghost.

'The lawn!' she gasped.

I rushed to the window but it was still there and I could see nothing unusual.

'It needs cutting,' she explained.

That was something of an understatement.

'Too late now,' I informed her. 'It'll soon be dark, there's the milking, and it's Friday. Not enough time.'

'Something must be done,' she declared in tones which brooked no argument.

I was inspired. Why not run the flock in for the night and let them eat off the grass? By the time they finished it would be neat enough and smooth enough for croquet. She looked distrustful. 'Really?'

'Would I lie about such a thing?'

She nodded 'Yes,' but could offer no alternative.

It took only a few minutes to bring in the sheep, all 135 of them, because, of course, the eight orphaned lambs were still refusing to mix with their common relatives. The woolly mass trooped past the house baaing and calling and I shut the garden gate behind them feeling distinctly pleased with myself.

Next morning the garden was like something out of a 1914–18 war movie. The sheep had eaten just about everything that could be reached. The roses, the honeysuckle, the blackcurrant bushes, had all been pruned down to the knuckle. Even worse: I had forgotten a bed of lettuce the kids had planted in a disused flower border. The sheep had not ignored it. They had also reared on their hind legs to munch low-hanging boughs of cherry and apple trees.

Nothing, except one thing, had been missed. They had scorned the grass. But in lieu of eating it, they had fouled up the lawn very, very thoroughly. It would need an issue of wellingtons before our friends could be taken out there.

Shirley let out an 'Eek' when she saw the scene. She became so agitated I began to think our guests were to sleep out on the grass and not be allowed indoors.

'They'll probably not even see the lawn,' I said to soothe her. It was wasted effort.

As it happened everything went very well. Our friends arrived more concerned about what the lane might have done to their exhaust than the state of our garden which had not yet become public knowledge. They thought the house was very nice, which it was, admired the livestock and allowed themselves to be dragged on a safari round the boundaries of the farm. Robbie proved very adept at milking. Not one glimpse of the front garden did they get.

Next day, Sunday, we hurried through the work and took them on a tour of the locality, calling in at The Forge, and returning home for lunch. They were to leave for London in the early afternoon. It was only as they left us that Robbie spotted the garden.

'Sheep break in?' he asked sympathetically.

'Ruined months of work,' I informed him, accepting his condolences while Shirley did her best not to giggle.

They went off driving carefully up the stony lane which we had come to take so much for granted.

'See?' I said smugly. 'Everything was fine.'

It would have remained that way if my wife had been able to keep a secret. Instead, on the next foray we made to inner suburbia, she blurted out the truth. The revelation, with superb timing, came when Robbie, a dedicated gardener, was telling others of his ilk about my misfortune in having the sheep break in. Naturally the rustic Delilah had to make a public confession with suitable embellishments. I went from martyr to buffoon in one easy jump.

'Well, what do you expect from a simple country lad?' I asked and slunk out of the room.

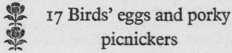

17 Birds' eggs and porky picnickers

The hawk hovered some twenty feet above the grass, sitting on the wind, watching for something to move on the ground below. It was a lean brown bird with lighter underside and a wingspan that must have approached three feet. It was, John assured me, probably a kestrel.

There is something fascinating about hawks. We took a brief rest from repairing a fence to study this one poised arrogantly above lesser creatures. A shower of sparrows left the safety of a nearby hedge and set out, flying low and hurriedly, across the field.

They were spotted before they had gone six feet. The watchful hunter singled one out, swooped down on the luckless bird and carried it to the grass. Half a minute later it took off again, carrying its kill to a gatepost to feed.

Since moving to Egerton and acquiring a 'spotter' book my family had begun taking an interest in the bird life around them. There was a lot to be seen from the pair of big tawny owls which lived in an old building on a neighbouring farm to the tiny red wrens nesting for the second year in a disused swallow's nest over the pig-sties.

Egg-hunters were not welcome so when the kids spotted a trio searching the hedges bounding the barley field, they came running to inform John and me. We called the dogs and went down to investigate.

They were teenagers, fourteen to seventeen years old by the look of them, all boys, well dressed and much of a likeness, tall and lanky, with pale Black Country faces.

'We ain't doing any harm,' the oldest of them protested when challenged. 'Just getting a few eggs. We collect them.'

'Not on this adjective farm, you don't,' John said emphatically. 'Get going.'

'There's footpaths we're entitled to walk on,' the same lad said defensively. 'You can't stop us.'

'There's no footpath along here,' I said. 'If you prefer, come along to the house and we'll call the police and see if they think you're allowed to take birds' eggs.'

The threat did the trick. They left promptly, if sulkily, making for the lane and then heading towards the road. It was a shame that three such youngsters should make the effort to visit the country and then set about destroying the very things that attracted them.

Summer had brought its usual quota of troublesome visitors. The idea that the countryside was something which could be pillaged with impunity was surprisingly widespread. In the cities if someone had walked into another person's garden and helped themselves, people would have been outraged. Yet ordinary people seemed to apply different standards to farmland and wildlife.

A father-son combination armed with an expensive, lethal-looking air rifle appeared in the top fields, potting at birds and anything else that moved. They looked genuinely surprised when we intervened and suggested they go elsewhere. The man produced a map and indicated the dotted public footpath which crossed the field. He considered that the presence of the path entitled them to poach and shoot round the place.

'You shoot, don't you?' he demanded when I disagreed, indignation making his well-fed face redden and swell.

'Not song birds,' I informed him. 'Besides, it's our land, we have the shooting rights, you don't.'

'Bloody selfish farmers,' he cursed, and led his son away to fresh hunting grounds.

When I related the story in The Forge, there were a dozen similar anecdotes. Everyone agreed that the vast majority of visitors came and went unnoticed, enjoying themselves, and not harming anyone or anything. It was the lunatic minority that soured relations.

'As long as they'll keep to where they'm entitled to go, close the gates and not drop rubbish where stock can get at it, it's not too bad,' someone said. 'But how often do they do it? There's more than one daft calf choked on a plastic bag. They'll pick them up and chew them for hours and then try and swallow them.'

There was general agreement with his sentiments.

What most of our friends did not appreciate was that to many townees the countryside was alien territory and ordinary farm animals could be frightening creatures. Just how true this was we saw when a family group, including two elderly ladies, decided to picnic in a corner of the field above the house.

John and I were fixing tiles on the steep roof of the milking parlour and had a perfect view of events.

'Better there than in the barley,' he said grinning, as they spread out a rug and brought out their food.

They were happy enough until our two sociable sows, Dorrie and Dorfie, who had been foraging in the gulley that ran along one side of the field, spotted them and went over to investigate.

The sight of the two big pigs soon dissipated the party spirit. The whole lot of them began waving their arms and shouting, but it had little deterrent effect. The pigs could smell the food. They grunted amiably; all they wanted to do was ingratiate themselves and share in the goodies. Even so they might have gone off but for a fatal error of judgement by the older man. He tried to buy them off by throwing a sandwich. It was like trying to douse a fire with petrol.

Before John could climb down the ladder and cross the field, the blackmailing pair had got through the best part of a plate of sandwiches.

I came up in time to hear the man, a pleasant enough looking type about my own age, accusing my son of having 'set them on us'.

'They're harmless,' the teenager told him. 'But if you feed them, they'll keep coming back.'

The party were not convinced. 'You all ought to be prosecuted,' one of the women sniffed. 'They'll kill someone one of these days.'

We suggested they might like to move into the adjacent field and close the gate on their unwanted guests, but they had had enough, off they went with their repacked basket, rug, and cloth, to sit in the safety of their car and eat.

John and I were sorry they had been frightened but the sows were unrepentant. Just as soon as we had left the corner and gone back to work, they charged across the field to see if anything edible had been left behind.

The occasional confrontation was a price we had to pay for living in a scenically beautiful area. In the main the seasonal flow of people came and went without disturbing anyone or anything, recognizing that what to them was a holiday area was also some farmer's workshop. The organized rambles were the least trouble, they trooped past, well-dressed and kitted, giggly girls and show-off boys, sometimes family groups with overfed dogs on leads, consulting a multitude of maps although the route was clearly defined. Some of the most venturesome would dare to smile and bid us 'Good-day'. We always touched our forelocks in what we thought was the true rustic manner.

It was particularly pleasing to see the young people who came down from the mountain laden with rucksacks, heading for the nearby Youth Hostel. By the time they reached Egerton they had come a fair way, having started from the far side and walked over the mountain. They still had slightly over two miles to go but some of them took a short-cut across the fields. No one objected, as long as they did no damage.

Slowly but surely, we were being converted to the cult of the bovine mammary gland. For the casual visitor to Egerton our little herd of bony, elderly Friesians might be just cows; for us they represented solvency, even a limited prosperity.

For the small farmer the big attraction of dairying is the regular pay cheque it brings. It was a great occasion when the postman came skidding down the lane in his little van bringing the monthly statement from the Milk Marketing Board which informed us how much, or how little, had been credited to our account.

With the summer grass the total was hovering about a respectable £250. True, a large proportion of this represented the cost of production, but, even so, it went a long way to justifying the discomfort of dawn rising and the seven-days-a-week grind.

Initially we had been content to try mixed farming with the accent very much on 'mixed'. We were anxious to gain experience and prepared to have a go at anything likely to bring in a few shillings. But as we progressed it was becoming increasingly obvious that any future for us must lie with dairying, if not in specializing completely, at least in greatly increasing that element of our effort.

Naturally Ellis, the little cowman who had introduced me to the mysteries of milking, had never doubted that we must, eventually, see the light. Given a free hand he would rapidly have cleared the farm of other animals and replaced them with dairy cows. But other friends counselled caution. Experience had made them conservative and taught them not to do anything without giving it a great deal of careful thought.

'Just you keep going steadily,' Howard advised. 'Keep adding cows but go carefully. Keep a bit of everything for the time being ...'

The rising milk cheque dazzled my family. Everyone became involved in making plans for the future, doing sums on scraps of paper, arguing, usually arriving at something wildly optimistic or terribly depressing. In the ultimate the bank statement would say it all but we were determined, once a chink of light appeared in the overdraft, to produce more milk. It was rather amusing when our suburban friends came visiting. They deplored the cost of clothes, cars, rail travel, colour television; we were equally shocked at the rising price of cows.

Whereas in our city days we had scoured the sales for furnishings or clothes, now we shopped around for cows at bargain prices. It soon became evident that the most likely sources were dispersal sales involving small farms. When big herds were on offer they attracted established dairy farmers with pockets far better lined than ours.

For our local friends sales were a combination of entertainment and business. They loved 'trading' – and went to great pains to keep us informed of forthcoming attractions.

Thus one morning in early summer Howard and I set off in the 1800 heading for a small farm so close to Wales it was in danger, according to my companion, of 'falling over the border'. Neither of us had been there before but the route was signposted from the main road. A twisting, narrowing lane climbed steadily up into the hills leading to a neat, stone-walled farmyard.

'Not too many folks here,' Howard commented as we parked. 'Might be one or two things will go cheap.'

First stop was the office – in the dairy – to collect a brochure and sales catalogue. The buildings were old but carefully maintained. The squat, stone-built farmhouse was separated from them by a high wall and sited in a holly-hedged garden. Howard and I leaned on a gate and studied it. There was about it the air of belonging that some buildings achieve with age.

'That's a house that's seen a few blokes come and go,' he said.

There were nine dairy cows in the sale and we went to the cowhouse to look at them. They were halter-tied, chomping their way through the hay provided to keep them happy, much of a likeness, Friesians with a suspicion of Ayrshire about them. Not as heavy as most of the Egerton cows.

'They'm a bit thin,' Howard said. 'But that's to be expected. In a place up in the air like this they'll have scraped the fields for feed. Get them down to Egerton and they'll do well.'

A friend of Howard's, a short, sturdy man with a red face and a wild mop of ginger hair, joined us as we walked round.

'This is David Griffiths,' Howard said and we shook hands.

'What are you two looking for?' the newcomer asked.

'A cow or two for Jacky, if they'm cheap enough, anything that's given away,' Howard informed him. 'You'm looking for junk, I suppose.' Griffiths laughed. 'There's an anvil I'd like.'

It seemed a peculiar interest. 'Are you a blacksmith?' I asked.

'Just a hobby. Now and again you'll see things that might be worth keeping: horse ploughs, hay-rakes, seed fiddles, things the wives used to use ... There's a barn filled with rubbish at my place.'

'Don't be taken in,' Howard said. 'His farm is like a museum. One of these days it's going to be worth a fortune.' He obviously approved of the other's interest.

The red-haired man explained. 'Not much hope of that happening but you go around and keep your eyes open, you'll see things thrown out as scrap that ought to be kept. One day we shall start looking around and the past will all have gone.'

'Is there a market for it?'

'Not really. I sold an old single furrow horse plough to be used as a pub sign. I've had one or two bits of luck like that but it needs to be set up properly, put on show so that the kids can see how it was.'

He proved unlucky when the sale began. The anvil went to a sportily dressed woman who paid out £35 and would have given more.

Griffiths knew her. 'At least it won't be destroyed,' he said. 'She's an interior decorator. That anvil will be sprayed silver or bronze and set up like a statue.'

Apart from the anvil the sale produced a run of low prices.

'Not much money here,' Howard observed with considerable satisfaction.

But things began to pick up when it came to the livestock. It appeared we were not the only people looking for bargains. The cows in milk went for prices around £125–£130, which we did not think cheap. Our luck changed when a thin but healthy cow, heavily in calf and dry, was run into the ring of straw bales in the stockyard.

Bidding was slow and reluctant and, prompted by Howard and Griffiths, I ended up getting her for a give-away price of £86.

'You can't lose on that,' Griffiths said. 'Take the calf and put her into the fatstock if she's not worth keeping; the butchers will give £100 for her, I'll bet . . .'

When we went into the cowshed to look at her more carefully, the farmer who was selling up was there. He was a pleasant old man, worn with work, neat in his best sports jacket, flannels and brown boots. 'Taking a last look before they go,' he said rather apologetically. 'You'm the bloke that got my little Moggie cheap.'

'I'd have gone a bit higher.'

He laughed. 'I'm not complaining. It takes two to make a deal. She's a good sound cow. That's her fourth calf in there and it's a good bull so it should be reasonable. This little girl is quiet as a mouse. The Missus reared her on the bottle and she'd follow us about.'

'Where is the Missus?' Griffiths asked. 'I haven't seen her about.'

The old man smiled ruefully, the mask slipping a little. 'She couldn't face seeing things go. She's away with a sister up in Wales until it's all over.'

'Have you got to sell?'

'No point in struggling on. My son's not interested. He's got a good job in town, good money, good hours, holidays. His wife is a town girl and doesn't want it. They'm not like us. We come here just after we were married . . .'

'You staying in the house?' Howard asked.

'No, no, the place is sold, the incomer wants the house for himself. We've a bit of a place down in the village. We'll move down there and enjoy a bit of peace.'

'I wish you well,' Howard told him.

I had been worrying about getting the cow back to Egerton but the problem was solved when another of Howard's friends came up and shook hands. He had a stock trailer behind his Land-Rover and was going back empty. For a couple of pounds he would call in at Egerton and deliver the cow for me. No trouble for him except to add a few miles to his journey. He backed the trailer into the yard and we loaded the cow and fastened her in. I handed over the cash and the man, grinning like a Cheshire cat at the unexpected business, set off.

Howard, the red-haired man and I followed more leisurely, stopping at the village café-shop-post office for a cup of tea. When we parted, Griffiths said, 'Bring the Missus over some day, Jacky, if you'm interested. There's a few bits and pieces worth looking at.'

'There's a bloke with two heads,' Howard said as Griffiths drove away. 'One stuffed with books and the other with common sense.'

Before I arrived home the cow had been delivered and was grazing quietly with the herd in the Top Field. They accepted her without the usual pushing and bullying, perhaps because she was a gentle, peace-loving creature. On Egerton's heavier grass she thrived and put on weight and her coat acquired a new sheen. Then one morning, about two months after her arrival, John collected Shirley and me and led the way to the Twelve-Acre.

Moggie's calf had arrived. It was a healthy, black bull calf and was already nuzzling and suckling. The cow looked at the three of us and then led her calf away to the far side of the sloping field. Perhaps she sensed that we would take him away.

Howard saw the calf two days later when it was being bottle-fed by Shirley and the kids.

'Anything over £50 for him will give you a gift of the cow,' he commented.

'She must be worth £140 now, if she's worth a penny.'

He was present a fortnight later when the calf sold for £54.

'Some 'as brains and some 'as luck,' he said.

'And some,' I told him smugly, 'know a bargain when it walks in front of them.'

19 A left-handed cow and a bumblefoot

It took the sale at Scrivener's Farm to drive home just what an old farmer had meant when he declared in the pub one evening, 'Having knowledge is all very well . . . but knowing how to use it; that's like having a handful of silver.'

It also successfully demolished a growing conceit on my part that I was beginning to approach my friends in understanding animals.

By the time Ellis the Cowman and I arrived the farm was crawling with folk. We were there because the little man had been a friend of the farmer whose sudden death had caused the sale.

'Gaffer Lewis knowed cows, there'll be no bad 'uns here,' he said as we parked Old Lil. He looked very dapper in a flat cap and a baggy tweed suit I had not seen before.

All very well perhaps, but there seemed little hope of finding cows to match my pocket when we joined the procession of men inspecting the herd which consisted of forty Friesians and two doe-eyed Jerseys kept for their extra creamy contribution. They were all housed in a long, low cubicled shed and tethered in two rows separated by the central dunging aisle along which we moved.

In the main the cows treated all the attention with bovine indifference, concentrating on the hay in their feed troughs or content to stand chewing the cud with a lazy, sideways movement of their jaws. The exception was a young animal which resented anyone and everyone coming near and kicked viciously at any man brave enough to lay a hand on her. Perhaps the noise had upset her. Whatever the explanation, there were some wry jokes about her reactions by characters who had experienced near misses.

'My word, I've seen a few wild 'uns in my time, but this'n'll match the worst,' a man who had dared to touch her udder told us shakily.

Another man laughed and agreed. 'She's a bit mad, if you ask me. Someone else can have her – I've got enough trouble at home without buying more.'

My feeling exactly.

A heavy, balding individual, sweating profusely although he had discarded his jacket to show a none-too-clean blue shirt, was in charge. He had been employed by the dead man and knew Ellis.

'The cows wasn't my work,' he told us. 'Gaffer looked after them hisself. You'd hardly dare put a foot in here when he was around.'

'What's wrong with her?' I asked, indicating the bad-tempered cow.

'Gawd knows,' he said helplessly. 'I'd a helluva struggle getting her into that bloody stall.'

Ellis reassured him. 'You've done them well. They'm turned out very nice.' His words were gratefully received.

The farmworker and half a dozen other men, including myself, watched apprehensively as my friend approached the cow and laid a hand gently on her flank. His reward was a swinging kick which would have sent him spinning had it landed. There was an amused murmur from the onlookers and the farmworker demanded, 'If that bloke can't handle her, who the hell can?'

We left her and moved on. By the time we reached the far end there were eight 'possibles' marked in the catalogue. But my companion's thoughts were elsewhere. 'It don't fall in with what I know of Gaffer,' he said. 'You saw the cow and I saw the cow but there was summat more. I'm going back for another look.'

'Sooner you than me,' I told him.

He rejoined me in the tea tent where men of all shapes and sizes were tucking heartily into sandwiches, cakes, pork pies and plates of hot shepherd's pie dug out of a king-size cauldron.

'Make a mark against her,' he said quietly.

'Which one?'

'The wild one, the kicker. She ought to go cheap.'

'Not cheap enough, Ellis,' I told him feelingly. 'If that damned cow comes to Egerton, I'm moving out. It would be like a football match with me the ball.'

He nearly choked on a cheese sandwich.

'What can you have seen that's changed your mind?' I demanded.

'What do you think?' he countered.

I thought she looked demented: that was what I thought.

Before the cows were sold at the end of the day, I had acquired some pig troughs, three partly used rolls of barbed wire and a small tea-chest filled with odds and ends including some carpenter's tools and screwtop jars filled with carefully oiled nuts and bolts, screws, nails and staples.

'Gaffer was a man who believed in having everything in its proper place,' Ellis said.

We got a good position against the wooden rails of the paddock where the cows were auctioned. It was crowded with men who looked as if they had cut their teeth on milk churns.

From the moment the first cow came into the ring, bidding was keen. A fleshy, obviously knowledgeable gentleman in a khaki battle-dress top bought three of the first five cows offered at prices around the £170 mark. Two of them had been on our list but I never even got into the bidding.

However the eleventh to be sold was a grey-cheeked cow, dried off, giving no milk but due to calf in the near future. I bought her, not with Ellis's whole-hearted approval, for £115.

'It's milk we should be buying, not calves,' he admonished. 'But she looks a sound enough animal.'

There was a stir when No. 19 – the kicker – entered with a head-swinging rush and came to a fidgeting halt. One of the labourers tried to make her walk round by prodding with a stick. The result was something between a lateral cartwheel and a firecracker with feet. He retreated hurriedly amid loud applause.

Things were going well, the auctioneer was relaxed and happy with the prices being reached.

'Now here's a nice cow, gentlemen,' he joked. 'This is one for the Missus to handle. Sound from teeth to tail . . . and good feet. Shall we say £150 to start?'

Absolutely no interest.

'All right, you make the mark. Who'll say £130?'

No one would.

In steps he came down to £100. The man in the battle-dress top said something to his neighbour, half raised his catalogue but changed his mind.

'This is ridiculous,' the auctioneer said in feigned indignation. 'She's a fine animal. Who'll say £95?'

Ellis kicked my foot; I waved my catalogue almost in a reflex action.

'Now, here's someone who ain't afraid of a little cow,' the auctioneer told the crowd. 'Who'll make it £100?'

Battle-dress looked thoughtfully at Ellis but did not bid. Nor did anyone else.

'Going once, going twice, going three times. I sell to Mr Holgate.' The auctioneer slammed down his gavel and asked silkily, 'Which do you prefer sir, of Egerton or London?'

There was a general relaxation at the sly dig. For one long moment they thought they might have missed something. But 'London'? No wonder he had bought the kicker.

We watched the rest of the herd sold. The finale was provided by Gaffer's Hereford bull. He was a magnificent animal, perhaps a little elderly but every inch a pedigree.

'Now there's a beast,' my friend said admiringly.

Battle-dress had moved along the rails to us. Altogether he had bought eight cows but something was worrying him.

'Worth a bit?' he asked the little man.

'He never got a bad calf for Gaffer,' Ellis told him promptly. 'Gentle old boy too, which is worth a little bit in itself.'

'It is indeed ... and yet you bought that daft cow,' the other said quietly, voicing the doubt niggling within him. 'There was something I missed, wasn't there? What do you know that I ought to?'

'We both looked at the same cow,' Ellis told him, laughing, but refused to satisfy his curiosity.

The other looked inquiringly at me, but I could only shrug.

There was only one other serious bidder for the bull and Battle-dress got him for £385 which, everyone agreed, was a give-away price. But the buyer went off frowning and thoughtful, heading for the cowshed to take another look at the kicker. His professional pride had been bruised.

Once the sale had ended there was much to do. We went to the office and handed over a cheque. There were several hauliers present and a tall man with a stomach that bulged over his leather belt undertook to bring the two cows to Egerton but warned that it would be 'a mite late'.

Old Lil skidded about on the grass where she was parked but, eventually, made it to the gravelled drive and settled down. This often happened if there was no load to make the back wheels bite.

'Now explain slowly how we're going to cope with a mad cow,' I said when we had covered the first mile on the way home without Ellis speaking.

'Don't worry, I'll be there to welcome her,' he said, evading my question, and slumped into the seat, pulled his cap down further over his eyes and guarded his secret.

The stars were showing and the screech owls were haunting the meadows before the cattle lorry came trundling down the lane. Ellis had finished his own work and was waiting with Thomas, his son-in-law, John and myself for its arrival.

We unloaded both cows straight into the collecting yard, tipped the driver and watched him depart thankfully up the lane. Egerton was his last call of the day and he looked very tired.

My suspicion that we had laid out £95 unwisely made me tetchy. 'Now let's see how this magic is going to work,' I demanded of Ellis.

Thomas and he laughed. 'You're the owner, you try first.'

When it was put like that, I could not refuse.

There was some difficulty getting the cow into the right-hand stand the cowman indicated, but there were four of us and after a struggle we managed it and fastened the restricting chain behind her. The little man offered me a bucket about half filled with warm water and a sponge. 'Go on, wash her.'

Some chance! The moment I touched her a splayed, cloven hoof, big as a soup plate, sent me back out of reach. On the second attempt I managed to get my head tucked into her flank as Ellis had taught but next moment the bucket was smashed out of my hand and sent flying across the floor.

Naturally, the watching trio thought this hysterically funny. I did not. 'Let's see you try,' I snapped at Ellis. It had been a long day and my patience was wearing very thin. 'I'll bet you a pound you don't milk this one without getting kicked.'

'You're on,' he said promptly and indicated the opposite, left-hand milking position. 'Let's move her over there.'

'Why?'

He smiled with an innocence too good to be true. 'Why not?'

There was no problem moving the cow, she changed stands willingly. My own son, grinning like a hyena, handed him the bucket and water.

'Now, now, my love,' the little man crooned. 'Settle down, settle down, nobody's going to hurt you.'

It was astonishing! The wretched animal was clearly nervous but did not lift a foot as he worked and the milk began to flow through the pipes into the suspended churn.

'That's my good girl,' Ellis burbled as he took off the units and dipped her teats in an antiseptic solution to guard against infection. 'Off you go now.'

And he pushed the handle which opened the gate in front of the cow and released her to trundle, still munching concentrates, across the moonlit meadow to join the resting herd. The incalf cow followed her.

'One pound please,' he said, holding out his hand.

It was passed over with ill grace. 'All right, what's the explanation?' I demanded, conscious of being fooled.

By the way they were smirking, John and Thomas had been in the know all along but they held their peace while the winner tucked away his gains. 'Blind, Jacky,' he told me. 'Blind in the left eye, can't see a thing coming from that side, so when she's touched, out she lashes. Been that way since a calf, I shouldn't wonder. Gaffer would have known because she was reared on the farm. He must have put her into a left-hand stall and always milked her from the one side. No wonder that daft sod had so much trouble getting her into a right-hand stall. All you've got to do is see that she gets a left-hand stand; nothing else. You'll have no trouble with her.'

It was not quite as simple as that, there were one or two settling down problems, but experience proved him right. The Kicker, as she became known, was a valuable addition to the herd.

Naturally, Ellis relived his triumph and my discomfiture in The Forge for the benefit of his friends. 'They was all too busy looking at her feet to notice the eye,' he said happily. 'But I sensed there was something and spotted it when I went back for a second look. That poor bloke that bought the bull knowed he'd missed something but couldn't put his finger on it. Just as well, he'd have had her if he'd known and she's worth every penny of £170 now, isn't she, Jacky?'

I confirmed the valuation.

It was a coup which roused the admiration of Aaron, the burly gent who farmed up the mountain. 'By gum you'm the foxy one and no mistake, Ellis,' he said.

The cowman took that as a high compliment. 'Know what? If old Gaffer Lewis had been about he wouldn't never begrudge us that cow. He'd have laughed his eyes out.'

'He would that,' Aaron agreed. 'Gaffer was a real cowman and they'm born, not made. That's for a fact.'

And it was.

Not all our purchases were unqualified 'bargains'. One old cow cost £123 after a tussle with another farmer who thought she had been knocked down to him for £120.

'Sold to Mr White,' the auctioneer proclaimed, thumping his gavel down on the whitewood table set in the farmyard where the sale was being held.

It was a mistake. The last bid had been mine. Everyone around John and me rushed to our defence and pointed out his mistake in no uncertain manner.

'What's the matter? You wearing blinkers?' one hefty character, whom I had never seen before, shouted at the harassed man.

There was a re-run which ended with me getting the cow amid hearty cheers and to the obvious chagrin of my rival.

Alas, the triumph was blunted when we got the animal home and realized, for the first time, that she had a deformed foot. She had walked very deliberately when brought into the ring but neither of us had spotted the defect in the cowshed.

'Her's got a proper bumblefoot,' Ellis the Cowman said when he inspected her that evening. He had not been at the sale. Seeing my expression, he laughed. 'Nothing much to worry about, Jacky. I knowed a cow once that only had two tits. She'd lost t'others in an accident. This is a fair cow and she ain't going to run back home, that's for sure.'

Some consolation, perhaps, but it did nothing to help when the rest of the locals heard about it.

'Always count their legs,' Old Jonathon advised me gleefully. 'If they don't have four good legs, make sure they knows how to walk on a stick.'

By the next Monday market the story had got round with considerable embellishments.

'Never mind, I'll bet she's got nice manners,' Tall Stan, the friend I met at sales, teased.

In fact she proved a very equable creature and rapidly established herself as a favourite with the kids who named her 'Granny'.

The vet came in to pare the hoof which was something like an overgrown toenail and showed John and me how to fasten the cow's leg to the steel uprights of the milking stand and do the job ourselves. 'Nothing much wrong with her,' he said, packing away his instruments. 'She's sound enough but for the foot. Besides, what would vets do if every animal was perfect?'

Welcome, reassuring words, but then he spoiled them by adding, 'Mind, if you're going in for three-legged animals, better make sure they've got something to lean against or they'll keep falling down.'

 ## 20 A prickly problem

There are good days in farming, there are bad days ... and there are days not fit to be mentioned in decent company. This one headed the last category.

It began with the alarm failing to go off. My fault – I had forgotten to wind the clock – but that was no consolation. The lost half-hour robbed me of that vital cup of coffee which made facing the early morning world possible. Our schedule did not allow for over-sleeping.

The cows were grazing the Top Field. When I appeared, bleary-eyed and flustered, they looked at me accusingly and crowded through the gate, eager to be milked. The weather was good, the grass was green and plentiful, and their swollen udders told them, better than any timepiece, that I was late.

Once the heavy iron sheeting doors of the collecting yard had been slammed behind them, I scurried round trying to make up the lost time and finding that haste made me all fingers and thumbs with jobs that were usually routine.

As soon as the first cows were in position, I pressed the button to start the electric motor which drove the vacuum pump. There was a loud whirring noise but the pointer on the pressure gauge did not move. The drive belt had come off! It had happened before but now getting it back on seemed to take a lifetime. I rushed at the job and, as a result, it took twice as long.

Things began to improve once the machine was running. The milk flowed, the churns filled, I lifted the full ones on to my little trolley, lugged them into the dairy and set the water cooler spinning round, taking the heat out of the steaming liquid.

There were six full churns, a seventh was filling, and I was beginning to congratulate myself on an excellent recovery when Ermintrude's long, thin face appeared in the doorway.

Normally this was a welcome sight because our Ermintrude was always the last cow to be milked. She was a civilized creature who believed in peace and order. Not for her the scuffling and shoving of more boisterous herd mates. She was content to come in last when there was no hustle and a soul could take her time. Ermintrude was at the bottom of the pecking order, happy to be there and without ambition.

As soon as she was in position I went through the usual routine, washing her udder, giving each teat a quick squeeze to check that nothing was wrong. She fidgeted and lifted a back foot but settled down again.

The trouble began when I put the units on her. The vacuum

pump popped away steadily, the units tightened and relaxed rhythmically on the cow's teats, the milk began to flow.

Not for long though! Poor Ermintrude suddenly went rigid, for all the world like some upright spinster who has just had her backside pinched. Then she acted! One back foot swept the irritating units off and, in the shuffling about that ensued, they were trampled into the muck.

Now dairying is excellent training in self-control. Experience had taught me not to blow my top when such things happened. Nothing panics cows quite so quickly or thoroughly as the dairyman's voice raised in anger. Shout at one, you shout at the lot, and they all react.

So I gulped hard, retrieved the dirtied units, soothed the unhappy cow, and took the tackle into the dairy to wash it under the tap.

Nothing appeared to be amiss with her udder. No cuts, barbed wire wounds or bramble scratches. I replaced the units and held my breath. Ermintrude shrank away and tolerated them for nearly half a minute but then . . . off they came again!

Time was jumping along. The milk had to be taken to the top of the lane ready for collection at 8 a.m. sharp. There was nothing for it but to leave the cow in the stand and deal with her later.

John was up and about when I returned and put away the tractor. 'Why've you kept Ermintrude back?' he asked.

'Something wrong, she kicked the units off twice.'

He raised his eyebrows. 'Nothing I can see.'

The pair of us, very gingerly, inspected the cow's teats. It took a few minutes before his younger, keener eyes spotted the trouble. A cluster of minute thistle prickles, hardly visible, just protruding above the skin near the sensitive end of the teat. They must have been excruciatingly painful when the units were working. No wonder she'd lashed out.

The problem was how to remove them. My nails were blunt and broken; John's were not much better. The pincers we used to yank nails and bits of metal from cow hoofs were too crude but we tried them, and other methods, for nearly half an hour and got quick protests when we pinched her skin. Finally we decided to leave poor Ermintrude waiting even longer and seek inspiration over breakfast.

Shirley listened to our problem with widening eyes. 'Poor Ermintrude! Prickles there of all places!'

It required, she assured us, a woman's touch and promptly abandoned cooking our meal to go and succour the cow. Our protests were ignored; she led the way to the milking parlour equipped with eyebrow tweezers and a child's magnifying glass.

John gave me a nudge as the female Kildare bent to her task. Any moment now a threatening hoof must restore our masculine pride. But it was not to be. Ermintrude appeared to recognize the expertise and sympathy and stood patiently as Shirley located and extracted five bits of prickle.

'There,' my wife said, oozing self-congratulation, 'that's the last nasty piece.'

The cow turned her head and blinked self-pitying, long-lashed brown eyes at her benefactor. It was a touching scene!

There was nothing to do but milk the cow quickly, turn her loose and return to breakfast . . . and reconcile ourselves to hearing, again and again, just how a 'mere woman' had been forced to come to our rescue.

'She makes it sound more like a heart transplant than pulling out a few little splinters,' John complained when we were back at work again and out of hearing.

He was right: by the time it was told to our suburban friends it had all the drama of a TV serial.

We had trouble with the thistles throughout the summer. Cows and grass go together. The stuff they warn you to 'Keep Off' in municipal parks was our basic material and the more use we could make of it, the sooner would our bank balance stop bleeding to death.

Egerton had a reputation as a sound grass farm able to carry a high level of stocking but the prickly plants had established themselves at the top end of its seventy-five acres, particularly in the Camp Field, the little triangular field whose bumpy surface concealed a Saxon village. The weed had grown unchecked there for years. There were islands of thistles, so thick and strong that no animal could graze the area they covered.

This was a situation we could not accept. If we were going to survive we needed to use every inch of ground. We followed the local practice of taking the swathe board off the grass cutter and mowing them. Removing the board avoided the thistles being collected in rows like mown grass and left them lying where they had been felled. The snag was that even after this had been done, the seeds ripened and went parachuting away riding the wind. In addition the prickles of the fallen, drying thistles were a constant menace to the suspended milking equipment of our cows.

For £22 at a sale, I managed to buy a secondhand sprayer which fitted behind the tractor. It consisted of a square, heavy tank fitted with a pressure pump worked off the tractor and twin, seven-foot booms with nozzles at eighteen-inch intervals.

Our friends were rather sceptical at first but when they saw how effective a selective spray could be, they began to follow our example. Besides, it gave them a chance to borrow something from us for a change. John soon had a thriving business going whereby he charged one pound an hour for the use of the sprayer and his services.

It was a particularly pleasing moment when the farmer whose land adjoined the Camp Field leaned over the low, blackthorn hedge and asked how we had managed to control the pest.

'I can't recollect cows ever being able to use that field when the thistles were at their full,' he said.

He had thistle problems of his own. As soon as he said this, John acquainted him with the existence of the Holgate spraying service and promptly acquired a new client.

 21 A crisis with our milk

The solitary churn on the stand and the doleful face of Jock, the milk lorry driver, said it all. The dairy had rejected ten gallons of Egerton milk!

The stocky little man gestured towards the churn. 'I'm sorry Jacky, they pulled it out yesterday and it failed the test. There've been one or two churns sent back, perhaps it's the hot weather, perhaps you've got a cow with mastitis.'

A red label attached to the churn informed us that the milk lacked acceptable 'keeping qualities' and advised us, if the cause could not be ascertained, to contact the Ministry of Agriculture's local Dairy Adviser.

There was nothing to be done but hand over the churns I had brought up with the tractor and return with the 'failed' milk. It was the first time it had happened to us and it was a sickening moment.

My arrival with the news conjured up a sackcloth and ashes atmosphere. The three of us – Shirley, John and me – stood looking at the churn, trying to assess where the trouble might be. We were conscientious in washing the milking tackle. Each time it was used we brushed and scrubbed using sterilizing hypochlorite. Once a week everything was pulled to pieces and the whole lot, rubber pipes, metal 'claws' and 'cups', boiled in the dairy boiler. If anything we tended to overdo things, but our attitude was 'Better safe than sorry'.

Now this! It was like being accused of committing a public nuisance.

There were financial implications too. For a start we had lost the value of the ten gallons returned. Bad enough but, much worse, each month, on a day of their choosing, the dairy checked each producer's milk for composition, hygiene and antibiotics. Each month farmers were notified of the results of the test. Hitherto we had always received a clean bill of health, now we were obviously at risk.

A first monthly failure in hygiene brought a warning but no penalty. Succeeding failures brought an increasing reduction in the price paid for all the milk supplied during the month. What's more, six consecutive months with a clean record were required before the sequence could begin again with a warning but no penalty.

An even sterner view was taken when antibiotics were found present. They could be dangerous to consumers and also create problems in cheese-making. Two failures without penalty were allowed but afterwards a deduction of about twenty-five per cent was made on the whole month's supply of milk.

We were already in the last week of the month so the test result must be with us any day. It came, in fact, on the third day after the return of the churn. It was what we had feared most: failure! Everyone walked round in a daze of depression.

No good moping, we told ourselves, and set about trying to trace the trouble. Finally, and reluctantly, because it reflected on our efficiency, we decided to call in the adviser.

It was the same pleasant, no-nonsense ex-Land Girl who had approved our application to become registered as milk producers. 'Don't worry, I'll come along in the morning,' she said cheerfully over the phone.

My despondency caused Shirley to suggest that we walk to The Forge, but the possibility of meeting Ellis the Cowman and other friends kept me at home. If he had wheedled the news out of Jock or noticed the giveaway red label, it was going to take some living down.

The adviser's Mini came down the lane while we were still at breakfast. Shirley promptly provided her with a mug of tea and sat her down. 'It's not the end of the world,' our visitor laughed, noting the gloom. 'You'd be surprised the calls I get from people who've been farming all their lives. Ninety-nine times out of a hundred it's something simple that's been overlooked. You watch, you'll kick yourselves for not spotting it.'

No hanging about for this lady. Once her cup was empty we went over to the dairy and she bustled about taking the tackle to pieces and congratulating us on its cleanliness. Even so she took swabs and popped them into jars to be sent for a laboratory check.

Our milking machine allowed six cows to be accommodated line abreast with three being milked simultaneously. She went through it systematically, checking it point by point, taking more swabs, marking them, popping them into her glass containers.

Suddenly, the light dawned! It had to be the vacuum pump which was situated on the far side of the wall in the foodstore and reached by a heavy, ancient connecting door. It was the one thing we had overlooked and so obvious now, I did not know whether to curse or cry. A glance at John's face was sufficient to confirm that he had arrived at the same conclusion.

Our lady visitor began to laugh. 'Like to guess where the trouble is?'

Neither of us spoke. There were no words to express our feelings as she lifted off the bucket fitted into the line to protect the pump.

'We usually check it when we sterilize the tackle in the boiler,' I said in answer to her unasked question. 'It got missed this time, there's been a lot going on. It was my fault . . .'

'Didn't I say you'd kick yourselves?'

She shook the bucket so that its contents slopped about. A few cupfuls of milk had been sucked into the vacuum and ended up in the trap. It smelled foul. I went outside and poured it down a drain.

'We usually run a bucket of sterilizer through the machine once a week, sometimes more often,' I said limply.

Now we knew where the trouble lay, I knew what to do. Shirley provided some caustic soda and we stirred it into a bucket of hot water and used the vacuum system to draw it through the machine's pipes. Not once but twice.

'That should get rid of anything hanging about,' the adviser said. 'It's not to be recommended for too frequent use, it eats away the pipes, but this is something of a special occasion.'

Just to get it right out of the pipes, we ran through a couple of buckets of clean, warm water.

When it was all finished, the efficient little woman tucked away her swabs and samples and said, 'I'll send these to the laboratory and ask them to hurry things. We should get the results in a few days and I'll let you know. And I'll give the dairy a ring and ask them to do a special check on your milk.'

We must have looked apprehensive because she said soothingly, 'Don't worry. It'll be all right this time.'

A cup of coffee later she climbed back into the Mini and took off, heading for a farmer who wanted her advice on the provision of cubicles for his cows.

'How stupid can you get?' John demanded of himself and

everyone as she disappeared from view. 'Most times we'd have gone straight to the trap.'

There was nothing to do now but wait. Shirley took the call which told us the laboratory tests had found nothing, but we had moved into the new month before the young, red-faced postman handed over the small buff envelope containing the vital dairy results.

'First one to arrive this month,' he said and turned his van round.

John and I forced a nonchalance we did not feel.

'Let's hope that's a good omen,' I told him.

'Sure to be,' he said, 'although they do say bad news travels quicker than good.'

It took considerable restraint but we – Shirley had joined us – waited until he was driving away before I ripped open the envelope. What we were looking for was the last entry on the long, thin strip of paper. Just one word: PASS.

The relief was incredible. It was suddenly a new day. We abandoned ideas of work and went indoors to celebrate with a glass of Shirley's dandelion wine. She and Vicky had collected the yellow heads to make it in the spring. It could have done with a little more time to mature, but was pleasant enough and refreshing with a distinct 'tangy' flavour.

That same evening I called on Ellis to return some tools. He came out of a shed when he heard the car. His face crinkled into a smile and he said, 'Hello, we was beginning to think you was avoiding us or something.'

'Been a lot doing down at our place,' I told him evasively.

'Come and look here,' he said, turning into the shed.

The attraction was a newborn calf suckling its mother, an elderly Friesian. Its rust-brown coat was still birth damp and curly and the clear, limpid eyes looked enormous in the white face. The cow looked at us, decided there was no threat and went back to grooming the calf, using her big, rough tongue on whatever portion of her could be reached.

Ellis turned the calf round for my inspection. 'Nice, blocky little thing,' he said. 'She'll make a good beef animal. I've had the cow for years and she always throws a good calf.'

The cow and calf made an attractive picture and we stood watching them for some minutes, talking about this and that, but not milk failures.

'You've been having trouble, have you?' he asked.

'Nothing wrong,' I assured him. 'What makes you ask?'

He laughed. 'By gum, Jacky, you'll never make a good liar.' But he pushed the matter no further and walked to the car with me.

When I drove away he was standing in the middle of the yard, stroking the side of his nose with one thin finger, smiling at something unspoken.

 ## 22 Warbles and Rufus goes blind

One quiet, dozy afternoon in late July the dairy cows appeared to take leave of their senses. Twenty staid, seen-it-all cows suddenly began galloping about the field, tails held high, udders swinging alarmingly, racking their bony frames for an extra yard of speed to escape something chasing them.

No need to speculate about what troubled them; they were running from the Warble fly. This wretched insect, something like a bee, lays its eggs on the poor beasts, preferably among the hair of their legs or underbelly. They hatch and the larvae then proceed to eat their way right through the animal until they appear under the skin of the cow's back the following spring. These parasites bore a hole to breathe and finally eject, fall to the ground, go through the pupae stage and produce more unwanted warbles to start the whole round again.

No wonder the cattle feared them. The sight or sound of the fly approaching or hovering was the signal for quick exodus.

Our first contact with the repulsive warble had been in the

previous late spring when I ran my hand along the back of one of the cows – Lizzie-Three-Spots – as she was being milked and found a row of four sizeable lumps.

Shirley came in while I was examining them and asked, 'What are they?'

'Boils or something like that,' I told her and experimentally squeezed the biggest.

Her eyes popped with horror as a great, grisly grub some three quarters of an inch long and fat as a pencil slowly emerged. When I placed it on the palm of my hand and rolled it about, she shrank back in disgust. Poor Lizzie obviously resented attempts to produce the occupants of the remaning lumps, so I gave up and popped the grub into a matchbox to show in The Forge later that evening and see what could be learned about it.

When I arrived at the pub, mine host, the plump, worthy Griff, was building up the open fire. The jacket of his blue serge suit had been hung on a wooden peg driven into the white-painted stone wall to avoid it getting dirtied, and he was in waist-coat and shirt sleeves. Old Jonathon and half a dozen of his cronies were offering advice but no assistance.

Griff dropped the last of an armful of logs on the blaze and winked at me. 'If that don't warm you Jonathon, there's nothing except a good woman can and you'll have to find her for yourself,' he told the old man who had obviously been complaining. 'If you'm still cold, perhaps you ought to try running about a bit.'

'Run about? Me? For Gawd's sake, Griff, can't you see I'm all but crippled for life? Didn't that cow stamp on my foot bad enough nearly to take it off?'

'It was a calf, barely a month old,' his brother Matthew, who was sitting alongside the sufferer, told everybody. 'If you'd have heard him yelling, you'd've thought the devil 'ad him.'

That, Old Jonathon could not accept. 'It was the cow, not the calf, you fool.'

His brother busied himself with his pint mug to hide a grin.

'Now, Jacky,' Griff said, putting his jacket back on, 'what can I get for you?'

One of the cronies, a little man with a thick, greying moustache, insisted on treating and brought me beer in a pewter tankard. 'There'll be a place for a centre-forward in the village football team next Saturday, if we canna get Jonathon fit,' he said, laughing.

Having lost a couple of toe-nails by being trodden on by cows, I was inclined to be a little more sympathetic. So I refused to join in the baiting and produced the matchbox and grub. 'Seen one of these before?'

It was passed from hand to hand before Matthew asked, 'Do you want it?', and slung it into the fire when I shook my head.

'I just want to know what it is.'

'Gad-fly,' Old Jonathon said. 'Warbles, some calls them. Same thing. If your cows have got'um, best get a tin of dressing, mix it up and pour it along their backs. That'll get rid of them. It kills 'um afore they can get out into the air, while they'm washing around inside the beast.'

'That's about it,' Griff confirmed. 'There was a lot of flies about last summer and now the grubs is coming through.'

'Here!' the little man who had bought the beer asked suddenly. 'You don't think Jonathon's got the warble?'

That caused a laugh, but Old Jonathon said feelingly, 'I wish I had a good foot. It wouldn't be no football I'd kick.'

The next morning Shirley came with me when I drove into town to buy the necessary dressing which came in a powder form and needed to be mixed with water before being applied. There was no difficulty getting it and the local Farmers' Cooperative store supplied an explanatory leaflet as well.

We did some shopping and then had lunch in a neat little café in the shadow of the tall-spired church; meat and two veg, apple pie and custard. My wife was rather subdued and thoughtful. On the drive home she read about the life cycle of the fly and was plainly more horrified than ever.

Back at Egerton she busied herself with the textbooks which provided what farming knowledge we did not scrounge from the locals. It was unlike her to sit reading when there were a dozen things to be done, but no explanation was forthcoming until, greatly relieved, she replaced the books on their shelf in the end lounge and announced, 'Well, thank Heaven for that. We're safe. Warble flies do not attack people!'

There were far worse tribulations awaiting us. Rufus, the red calf, was going blind. The announcement by the vet quite shattered Shirley. She had reared the little animal from birth and, like the rest of the calves, it regarded her as a sort of surrogate mother. The sound of her footsteps in the stockyard was sufficient to set the calves bawling hopefully at the doors of their pens. John and I could come and go without bothering them, but my wife had only to join us and speak and the four-footed babies demanded her attention. Nor, as they grew into hulking creatures, did they forget. It never ceased to amuse our local friends to see the animals come running when she called. Mind, it was inviting reprisals to refer to her, as the kids sometimes did, as 'the calves' mother'.

Like most young animals, the calves responded eagerly to sympathetic treatment. It was generally accepted locally that women 'had a better way' with calves and many of them took on the 'rearing' in addition to their many chores. On Egerton Shirley's only rival for the calves' affection was Vicky who equally enjoyed fussing and feeding them.

The vet's visit followed the appearance of a film over Rufus' right eye. 'New Forest disease,' the tall, dark Welshman pronounced. 'I'll leave you something to drop into his eyes. I doubt if you can save the one eye but we might be in time to keep the other.'

'What if he goes totally blind?' Shirley asked.

He shrugged. 'They have been reared but you've got to pen them up altogether.' The disease, he said, was fly-borne. It was contagious and we would need to keep a close watch on the rest of the young stock.

'Will the eye always look so bad?' Shirley asked. It was an unpleasant sight.

'The film should clear away, but it'll leave a dead pupil,' he told her. 'There's a lot of it about. You take a look round the auctions, you'll soon spot cattle that've had New Forest.'

He was a pleasant man, always over-worked and apt to get

short-tempered because locals had left it too late before calling him in. 'They expect you to bring a beast back from the dead,' he said bitterly on one such occasion. 'By the time they pick up the phone, you might just as well knock the suffering thing on the head and send for the knacker's man. It's much too late, a waste of time and energy.'

At least we were not guilty of that fault and he had been successful with a number of our animal patients.

'No good worrying, Mrs Holgate,' he told Shirley as he handed over various bottles and packets and gave instructions about what must be done. 'I'll pop along and keep an eye on things whenever I'm in the neighbourhood and you phone me if there's a need.'

For the next few weeks Shirley and Vicky conscientiously treated the calf, but Rufus drooped like a flower and went off his food. Nothing seemed to stimulate his appetite or give him the will to live. Finally, he simply died.

'Pneumonia,' the vet said. 'But that was just at the end. There's really no satisfactory explanation for a case like this. Some animals will fight back to health when you'd think it was just a matter of digging a hole; others will suddenly lie down and die. Sometimes I think the calves miss the cow.'

He was sympathetic but it was something he encountered almost daily, whereas for Shirley and Vicky it meant the loss of a pet as well as a farm statistic. Myself, I had reservations. The work involved in rearing a blind calf to a finished beef animal, about a two-year job, would have fallen largely on Shirley and she already had more than enough to occupy her waking hours. However, I knew better than to express such sentiments in front of Egerton's two ladies. They would have denounced me as heartless. Perhaps they were partly right. I was aware of a change of attitude towards such matters. Time and effort were limited, precious commodities, not to be expended on hopeless projects.

'You'm beginning to think like a real farmer,' Old Jonathon would have said had I told him. I did not; I preferred to keep my own counsel.

The first thing I knew about the village show was a yellow poster tacked to a twisted ash tree by the roadside. It announced a whole day of attractions ranging from show jumping, pony competitions, and stock judging, to handicrafts, guess the cake weight, balloon racing, Punch and Judy, and a mammoth raffle with prizes galore.

Most impressive, I considered, but when I carried the news home, Shirley simply sighed her exasperation and said, 'You're so wrapped up in the farm everything passes you by. Everyone has been talking about nothing else for weeks.'

'Then how come I wasn't told?' I asked.

This was considered exceedingly comical. Vicky disappeared into the end lounge and returned with a handout which was virtually a replica of the poster. I took it off to read in peace.

August was the favoured month for shows in our area. The hay was in, the barley not quite ready, and the stock were out on grass; there was time to relax.

Once attuned to the idea of a show, I realized that Shirley was right; everyone was talking about it. Indeed, a lot of our friends were among the main organizers and no one was allowed to opt out.

'The Missus'll be entering summat in the garden produce section likely,' Old Jonathon said confidently when we talked over a stile at the bottom of the Twelve-Acre where our farms touched.

'I think we've eaten the best stuff,' I told him. 'She's a good cook so perhaps she'll bake a cake.'

He sniffed and looked disappointed. 'Horticulture's always the best stall, everybody says so.'

Howard, our ex-sergeant friend, laughed when I told him. 'Jonathon's biased because he organizes the vegetables. Wins most of the prizes, always 'as done. The Missus had better find summat or he'll be upset.'

'What about you?' I asked.

He looked rather surprised that I did not know. 'Shooting. Air rifles. What else?'

'What else?' I agreed. 'Do you want me to do anything?'

'You could give summat, say a pound, to the Fund,' he said and produced a crumpled receipt book and relieved me of a treasured note.

It emerged gradually that Shirley and Vicky between them planned to enter half a dozen competitions, most of them organized by Willem's wife. They fancied their chances with crab-apple jelly and knitting. Nick was making holes in his fingers trying to stitch together a grotesque suede animal which he fondly imagined looked like a pig. John, like me, was rather bemused.

'Now where are we going to find vegetables?' my wife asked indignantly. 'The moment anything reaches a reasonable size, we eat it.'

'Let's buy something at the market and enter that,' John contributed. 'No one will know.'

'It would be cheating,' Shirley said righteously. 'Besides, we'd be found out.'

'Not if we didn't win,' I said, seizing on the idea. 'We buy, say, a couple of cabbages, not particularly good ones, enter them, lose, bring them home and eat them. Everyone's happy, especially Old Jonathon.' It sounded hollow, even to my ears.

Shirley got up from her chair. 'Let's go and look round the garden. There might be something respectable enough to enter.'

There was nothing.

The Monday before the show, which was on a Thursday because this was early closing day for local shops, I yielded to temptation at the market. There were some healthy-looking cabbages going cheap. I bid, got four in a cardboard box and, helped by John, headed towards the van to hide them.

No sooner had we got outside the building than we met Howard who said, 'Sell us a couple. We've got cabbages big as a Bobby's head but there's no looking at 'em, never mind eating them, they'm being saved for the show. Same with you?'

'Something like that' I lied.

Clearly that was the end of the planned deception. We handed over two and walked with him to the car park. On the way home John said philosophically, 'They wouldn't have had a chance by the sound of it.'

Perhaps not, but they could have saved a friendship.

It was against this background of growing desperation that Nicholas suddenly announced his intention to enter for the runner bean competition.

'With what?'

The six-year-old frowned at our ignorance. 'There are beans in my garden.'

There was a threatening move in his direction and he conceded and led the way through the stockyard and over the fencing round the pig compound.

Someone in the long-ago past had built a trellis to cover the wall which faced south on to the barley field. It was the warmest place on the farm and there was a story that at one time vines had been grown at Egerton and wine made. The soil at the foot of the wall had certainly been cultivated in the past and a number of pot-holes showed where Nicholas had been busy trying to grow things ranging from thistles to radishes.

There were no traces of vines but, far better, the trellis was bedecked with broad-leafed runner beans, complete with red, bee-visited flowers and, salvation, fourteen long, healthy beans.

'Enough for two separate entries,' John commented.

The young gardener was pacified with promises that one of the entries would be in his name and any prize money would be his.

When he was informed of our intentions, the old man was delighted. If we would get the beans to him on the Thursday morning, before half past nine, he would do the rest.

The great day dawned grey and overcast but Providence knew better than to risk a confrontation with Old Jonathon and his friends. By mid-morning the sun was doing his duty and by the time we set off, just before lunch, the weather was well-nigh perfect.

Our first view of the show brought a surprise; it was far bigger than we had imagined. The site, made available by the local estate, was alive with people and the number of cars indicated that the 'outsiders' from the neighbouring towns were present in force. Like us, many had brought picnic lunches, and one area, where the ground swelled into a gentle mound, was set aside for the purpose and dotted with family groups enjoying open-air snacks.

The eye of the show was the ring where the stock judging and horse and pony events would take place. Its perimeter was neatly defined by linked sheep hurdles broken only by the entrance and exit. Along one side ran a long, continuous canvas-covered construction housing various displays and stalls. Another side was dominated by an enormous marquee containing BAR and TEAS and REFRESHMENTS.

A third side, that nearest the car parking, had been allocated for livestock pens. We walked there first and admired and criticized the pedigree rams, milking cows and heifers.

But the main attraction was the great stock bulls, each nosering tied in its own little sacking-sided stall. There were three blocky, short-legged Herefords, 'dripping with meat' as Shirley put it, shampooed, combed and pampered until not one hair was out of place. Their rivals, as a breed, were represented by two enormous white Charolais bulls, impressive-looking creatures with an aura of strength and power about them.

Two men, obviously butchers, were comparing the animals. 'They'm the coming breed,' the taller of the pair, a balding, elderly man ventured, referring to the Charolais.

His companion, a slimmer, corduroy-suited gent, disagreed. 'Never; too much bone. And they gets too big a calf for the good of the cow.'

The whole area was spattered with caravans, stalls and displays advertising farm machinery, various services, insurances, animal medicines, clothing, fertilizers, pesticides, farmhouse furnishings; you name it, it was there.

In one corner harassed salesmen were trying, hopelessly, to drag a swarm of young boys off tractors and implements they hoped to sell to the lads' fathers. Nicholas recognized some of his school friends and left us at the gallop, with his mother shouting after him, 'Lunch in half an hour.' A minute later his fair hair identified him as the pretend-driver of a shiny new red-painted, powerful Massey-Ferguson tractor.

Shirley had been optimistic about the mealtime. We took three-quarters of an hour to reach the horticulture stall via a route which included a couple of abortive goes costing ten pence a time on Howard's air rifles, aiming at target cards with a prize promised for a clearly unattainable score.

'No one's managed it yet,' he informed us, after we had given up. 'Nor likely to. I've diddled the sights a little bit.'

Old Jonathon looked like something out of a pre-war British film, very gentlemanly in his Edwardian green tweed suit, high collar shirt and string tie. He must have been baking hot.

'Great news,' he said happily and led us to where our beans were on show. 'Fourth prize; twenty-five pence.'

'Marvellous,' I said. 'When's the pay-out?' It was obviously an indelicate question.

'There's an entry fee of ten pence. Two entries; twenty pence. Do you want the five pence or shall we give it to the Fund? All profits goes to hospitals, y'know, after we've set something aside for next year's show.'

John rolled his eyes. 'Better let the Fund have it and name a ward after us.'

Our friend nodded happily. 'You'm a sensible lad, John. Matter of fact I knew you'd say that; they've already marked it down as a donation.'

He bustled off leaving us looking at one another, wondering who was going to break the news to Nicholas.

Before we could move another familiar face came up and sold us raffle tickets – ten pence each, book of six for fifty pence. We were clearly expected to, and did, take a book.

'What's the first prize?' I asked.

'Little babby pig given by a woman up towards the ford. There's other prizes of course, but the pig's the only one worth winning.'

Shirley groaned. 'If we win, let's hope we get the second prize.'

We continued our rounds. The Holgate women did very well

in the competitions with a first prize for crab-apple jelly, a second for knitting – a sort of woolly nightie for a baby – and another second for Vicky's embroidery. Nicholas's suede pig was exhibited but unplaced. It lay, looking like a four-legged, mis-shapen pin-cushion, among a score of beautifully made handi-crafts. We pretended to have no connection with it.

Strangely, the women of the family had no trouble collecting their prize money and tucked it into their purses, looking very smug.

'We've given the entries to the Fund,' Shirley explained when I mentioned the magic word 'donation'.

That was no sacrifice; who in our family could have worn a baby's woolly nightie?

It was well into the afternoon when we finally unpacked our lunch; the show ring was filled with children riding ponies of assorted breeds and sizes, doing impossible things without falling off and whooping like marauding Indians. My feet ached. I col-lapsed thankfully on the grass and was wolfing down ham and cheese sandwiches when Aaron, who farmed up the mountain, arrived carrying a big basket and accompanied by a handsome, rosy-cheeked greying-haired woman of considerable poundage who could only be his wife. 'My Missus, Ria,' he announced proudly, indicating the lady.

'That's Shirley, my Missus,' I said. 'Vicky, daughter, John, son. We're just going to eat, sit down and have something.'

'Thank you, we will,' she said in a voice that was pure Welsh, and sank down with a grace that made light of her size.

'Ria?' I said. 'That's an unusual name.'

She laughed. 'After Maria Marten in the Red Barn ... so my father always said but then he was as big a liar as Aaron.'

The burly man tried to look disapproving. 'Wait a minute ...'

'We've brought a few things of our own,' Ria said, ignoring him, and she proceeded to unpack enough victuals – cold chicken, sliced roast pork, homemade sausages, apples, a fruit cake and two home-baked cottage loaves – to feed a platoon. John and I promptly deserted Shirley's frugal offerings and began to eat our visitor's goodies.

Our generous friend originated from the Snowdon area which

we knew slightly from holidays in the years before we began milking cows.

'There's mountains so steep you'd fall over backwards if you let go,' Aaron contributed.

His lady giggled deliciously. 'Have you ever known such a liar?'

Ten minutes later we had more visitors – Howard and Dilys and Old Jonathon and their contributions.

'They'll have to manage 'uthout me for a few minutes,' the old man told us.

He had brought along two six-bottle packs of pale ale. The feast was beginning to spread over the field.

'Do you need any tickets for the pig?'

Everyone hurriedly assured him their pockets were stuffed with the things.

'It's all for the Fund,' he wheedled, but there was no response.

Nicholas and a batch of his friends arrived, sweaty and ravenous. They descended on the eats and gaps began to appear.

'Nice to see healthy children,' Ria said approvingly. Their own family had grown up and left home. 'Flown like blackbirds without a backward look', was how she put it. They hadn't flown too far; they all lived within a mile or two of her.

By the time the party broke up it took considerable effort to find renewed enthusiasm for the show.

'Let's simply wait for the draw and go,' Shirley suggested.

This was scheduled for half past three and it was already four o'clock. When it was announced, the winner was not a name we recognized. John laughed. 'Probably a townee. Wonder what he'll do with a pig?'

We were in the car, Shirley driving, when Old Jonathon came hurrying over with his employee, Big Billy, carrying a hessian sack. The big man had obviously spent his day in the beer tent. He gave Shirley, whom he much admired, a beatific smile and hoped she had enjoyed the show. In return she presented him with a napkin-wrapped pack of ham sandwiches which were gratefully received.

'Sop up the liquid,' she told me *sotto voce*.

Jonathon was rather breathless but he managed, 'Wait, we've got something for you.'

Both my wife and I knew what was coming even before Big Billy produced the 'babby' pig from the sack.

'Well there, isn't that nice little pig?' the old man asked.

It was a couple of weeks old, sausage pink, runted and with an ugly, protruding navel. It squeaked against the handling and Billy quickly gave it to Vicky who began nursing it.

'There,' Old Jonathon said. 'Do you want him?'

'OK,' I said, ignoring the warning signs from Shirley who would have to take on the bottle feeding. 'Thank you very much. It is a nice little pig.'

My acceptance was greeted with relief. 'I knowed you'd like him,' our friend said and held out a hand. 'Two pounds please.'

John turned his face away and I saw his shoulders heave.

'I thought it was a gift.'

Old Jonathon was hurt and showed it. 'If it was mine, it'd be free, Jacky. But I'd to buy him from the winner because he wanted cash and 'ad got nowhere like to keep a pig. Two pounds ain't much for a pig, and think, it's for the Fund.'

There was nothing to do but surrender and dig into my thinning wallet. 'For the Fund then. How is it going? Up to previous years?'

He folded the two notes and tucked them into a waistcoat pocket. 'We'm doing better than ever, Jacky. It'll be a record year. The pig's done his bit. I give the chap one pound for him, now you've gived two. And it all goes to the Fund.'

'You bloody old crook . . .' I began, but Shirley let in the clutch and interrupted. 'Goodbye, Jonathon, and thank you for the pig.'

And off we went with me fuming but everyone else thinking it was extremely funny.

As it happened, Horace, that was what the family called him, thrived on the substitute sow's milk that our women bottle-fed him. His navel tightened and improved and, eventually, we were able to put him in with a pen of weaners. He was weeks older, smaller than any of them, but not noticeably different except that when the kids called his name he would, momentarily at least, lift his nose out of the feed trough and squeak in acknowledgement.

24 Cashing lambs and a hobbling ewe

Farmers are puppets responding to strings the seasons pull. We were no different from the rest, except perhaps our movements were clumsier, not so practised, and we took longer to recognize the tugging of our masters.

Our stage, Egerton, was tiny, but did any cast ever play against a backdrop as magnificent as the mountain which rose across the valley from us? It dominated the landscape, making toys of homestead, village and town; men lived in its creases, quarrelling about the rich soil that collected there, deluding themselves they owned it; it had seen dark-haired Celt and sturdy Saxon come and go; now tractors crawled about its feet, and when they had gone, turned to rust and blown away, the mountain would still be there, unchanged.

The seasons played with the great mass, splashing it irreverently with colours, dressing it according to their whims. Winter capped it with a bonnet of snow, spring threw a cloak of knotted, grass-green gossamer over its bulk; summer hung it with rich, thick drapes of golden broom, curled bracken, may thorn and stunted oak; and autumn simply scraped the palette clean over the pointed peak and let the colours mix as they ran down the steep flanks.

The scene was changing now. The summer that had fattened the stock and filled the barley was receding, stealing away, leaving the platform to autumn, vagabond in copper and gold. The tiring year was draining the goodness from the grass, making it necessary to supplement the cows' feed with concentrates to maintain the milk yield.

In the fields the stocky, dark-faced Suffolk-cross lambs grazed beside their ewe mothers, unaware that it was not affection which caused us to prod their backs or lift them to guess their weights. Their season had come; it was time to cash them in.

The second Monday in August John and I selected the twelve

heaviest lambs, loaded them, gave Old Lil her fix of aerosol starting fluid, and chugged off up the lane.

By now we were hardened enough to respond with rude finger signs when more affluent friends in more affluent vehicles overtook us on the road, making a feast of it, announcing their triumph with derisory horns. Old Lil would get there in her own good time, not a moment before. The only thing was to relax and enjoy the countryside, see how others' efforts compared with our own. We thought we came out quite well . . . !

The market was on the outskirts of the town and we were part of a stream making towards it. By the time we arrived there was a queue of vehicles for the unloading ramps. Some of the drivers – burly, weather-beaten men in flannels and sports jackets – had climbed out, glad of a chance to stretch their legs, and stood around chattering. Many were familiar faces and we acknowledged one another by nodding without speaking.

At last the bigger of two cheerful market labourers, overalled and wearing thigh-high PVC leggings, signalled our turn and I backed the van up to the concrete step. The pair, with John's help, brought the lambs off, divided them into two bunches of six and ran them through a system of pens separated by swinging tubular steel gates, on to the big market scales.

An elderly clerk sitting in a tiny office read the gross weight indicated by the scales pointer, did some quick calculations, scribbled in a ledger and announced that Egerton's products averaged thirty-nine pounds carcass weight. Very satisfactory indeed.

Although all might appear confusion, within minutes of being unloaded our lambs had been weighed, recorded and run into two adjoining pens, and there was ample time to park the van and get a cup of tea before the selling began.

A bunch of our friends were crowded round one big plastic-topped table when we walked into the cafeteria. Tall Stan, whom John sometimes referred to as 'our market consultant' because we valued his advice, was one of them. He rattled his teacup to show it was empty and we carried a replacement to him.

They were discussing otters. 'You ever see one at your place, Jacky?' Stan asked.

We had not, although the area was laced with streams which should have been perfect for the animal.

'There,' Stan told the others. 'A few years ago there'd uv bin two or three pairs round Egerton, working them streams right back up the mountain. Now they'm gone. So I say they ought not to allow hunting. I won't have'm over my land. Foxes yes, otters no. I've not seen one for years.'

'They eats fish,' a plump, moon-faced man named Sam said. 'They'll kill ducks. Years gone, when I was a lad and walked with the hunt, I seed an otter kill a good, old dog; swum right underneath, took'm by the throat and pulled'm under, drowned him dead. They can be very nasty. I've heard it said they can break a man's leg, if they take him.'

'A big dog otter can be vicious,' another man confirmed. 'But even when they was there, you never seed them if you didn't look.'

'What do you think, Jacky?' Stan asked.

Matthew, Old Jonathon's brother with the arthritic back, smiled. 'Jacky doesn't even like us shooting birds.'

Everyone turned, astonished, to look at me. 'It was magpies,' I explained. 'Matthew shot a pair of magpies. I only said they didn't do much harm. It was wasting cartridges.'

The moon-faced one was outraged. 'No harm? They'll only peck out a lamb's eyes.'

'Not proven,' I protested, aware that Matthew had neatly trapped me. 'They'll certainly eat carrion, dead animals, but so will other birds, crows, buzzards . . .'

'I've seed a living ewe with both eyes taken,' a thin man whose neck hung with loose folds of skin said quietly.

'Magpies?' I asked.

'Likely . . . She was snared in brambles, lying helpless . . .'

The clanging of the bell that announced the start of selling saved me. Everyone gulped down their tea and went out to watch prices.

Matthew grinned maliciously at me. 'Put you in it that time, didn't I?'

Tall Stan stretched to his full six-and-a-half feet and asked, 'What pens have you got?'

'Two, thirty-nine and forty. They averaged thirty-nine pounds.'

'That's a good weight,' he said. 'If you'm lucky they'll bring in something like £10. Want me to watch them for you?'

'Please,' I said.

We walked, together with the limping Matthew, to the pens. My lofty friend had something on his mind. 'Otters, yes,' he said finally. 'But magpies? I'm not sure, there's bad things said about them.'

Our lambs fetched £10.50 each, both pens going to the same white-coated butcher who felt their fat tails and nodded approvingly.

'Prime lambs,' said Tall Stan, who had surreptitiously bid against him to push up the price.

'Yours?' the butcher asked him.

'Ours,' I corrected.

'About the right size, cut up to reasonable joints,' he said and hurried after the other buyers.

In the weeks that followed, right into October, a lot of families would enjoy Egerton lamb as we made our contribution to the market.

Something must have happened to panic this old ewe and send her tumbling over the edge of the gulley. She had never reached the rocky bottom fifty feet below; instead she was caught in a short-stemmed thorn bush growing out of the gulley side, twenty-odd feet down. She lay there suspended, for all the world like a trapeze artist caught in a safety net.

Normally sheep are as sure-footed as their goat cousins. You can see them nibbling happily on the sheerest mountain-sides or walking unconcernedly along the narrowest ledges even though one false step must be fatal. So it was a surprise when the kids came running with the news. They led us to a place in the fifteen-acre field from which the land fell sharply, just off the vertical, to the shallow stream running below. The wire-netting fence had been broken at the spot.

'A dog probably running the flock against the fence,' John said, basing his judgement on the angle at which the posts lay.

'There she is,' Nicholas said, leaning over an edge made sharp by erosion and pointing. 'How will you get her up?'

That was the problem in a nutshell. The ewe, a big, speckle-faced Kerry Hill, lay so still we thought at first she was dead, but then an ear twitched. Flies were busy, depositing clutches of eggs so that the maggots could feed on the dead animal which must result unless something was done.

Nicholas and Vicky searched for other possible casualties while John and I conferred about what to do. Finally we decided to try and get a rope round her and bring her up. Going down would mean forcing a way through the bush which was reinforced by brambles as thick as your thumb. John went off to bring the tractor, a wagon rope and any other tackle which might be useful.

The kids found nothing else and came back spreading their hands to indicate the fact. They were very excited.

'It will be a real rescue, just like television,' Vicky announced happily.

'Pity we don't have a helicopter.'

When John returned, we dragged the remains of a fallen birch tree to the edge to give a curved surface for the rope to turn over like a primitive pulley. Next step was to tie the orange-coloured nylon wagon rope to the tractor and drop it down to the bush. The ewe stirred and lifted her head when it touched her but made no attempt to move.

My older son grimaced. 'Don't like that, something's wrong.'

'She might be a bit stunned; it might not have happened long,' I told him. But we both knew she had been there for hours, probably all night.

I clambered down to her, digging my toes into the gulley's side and hanging on to the rope, the nylon harsh on the palms. On arrival I found one secure foothold among the bush roots and a less happy one among the tangled branches. Now I could see that the brambles were decked with wool where the ewe had thrashed about before giving up and accepting her fate.

Getting a rope round her was painful because of the thorns and awkward handling, but I managed and tied it behind her front legs. There was no reaction from the ewe. She lay inertly as I worked but her eyes followed me.

When all was ready, John who was watching – and criticizing – my efforts, started the tractor and inched away. The rope tightened, took the strain and, slowly but surely, lifted the ewe out of the bush and up the gulley side. Even as she went I could see there was something wrong with one back leg: it stuck out at an unnatural angle.

The final stage could have been difficult but John simply accelerated and dragged the animal unceremoniously over the edge to safety. She kicked feebly as the rope dragged her along the ground and Nicholas sat on her head to prevent her rising when the motion stopped.

My ascent was by much the same means. The rope down again, I was pulled up with one foot in the loop which had lifted the sheep, and scrambled over the edge.

No need to be a vet to see that the rescued ewe had broken a back leg a few inches above the hoof. The line of the break showed clearly through the skin.

'A good animal,' John said, feeling her udder and then pulling back her lips to look at her teeth. 'Pity to have to finish her, especially when the freezer is filled with fat lamb.'

It seemed worthwhile trying to mend the leg, so we lifted her into the tractor transport box and headed back to the buildings. Once there, with the ewe still in the box because it made a convenient operating table, we straightened the leg – not a sound from the sufferer – and splinted it with two bits of thin board, tying them with bandages and winding red adhesive tape round the lot to finish off. There were several patches of flyblow on her, mainly where she had been torn by branches, so we scissored away the wool and cleaned the shallow wounds with a carbolic solution.

We were fearful that if she lay down, she might not rise again, so we rigged up two rope slings using the wooden partition in an empty pen to hold her in a standing position. An old enamel washing-up bowl raised on a concrete slab put some meal within her reach. Finally we mixed a pint of glucose and water solution, added a tot of elderberry wine, and simply lifted her head and poured it down her throat.

'A Holgate cocktail,' John said. 'Guaranteed to cure anything from flyblow to insomnia.'

His optimism was greater than mine. However, perhaps the cocktail did work because there was a happy ending. A couple of hours after the splinting operation, the ewe suddenly seemed to appreciate that she was still alive and took a few mouthfuls of meal. By the second day she was beginning to struggle against the restraining slings so, with great trepidation, we released her.

She tried the splinted leg, just touching the foot to the ground, decided against it, and stood precariously balanced, undecided. Finally she made the effort and hobbled painfully forward to reach some water in a trough.

'She'll be all right,' said Shirley, who had come, aproned and floury handed, to watch. 'This one should live.'

We carried our patient into the front garden where she could graze the lawn and we could keep an eye open for complications. She was more interested in the meal than in the grass. On the fifth day we lifted her into the transport box and took her back to the flock. Once free she hopped towards them, slowly but determinedly.

'What happens if she lies down and can't get up again?' I asked.

John's eyes followed the clumsily moving animal. 'We shall have to get her to her feet, I suppose.'

It never happened. She was always upright and moved increasingly easily on three legs. About five weeks after the 'rescue' we deemed it safe to remove the splints.

They had, we found, worked loose and the leg had set crooked. There was a bulging lump where the bone had knitted together and for weeks afterwards she continued to carry the leg. Even when it was sound enough to take her weight, she was always discernible by her hobbling gait.

But it obviously did not interfere with the course of nature and the following spring she rewarded our efforts with two fine lambs. There was nothing wrong with their legs.

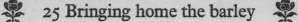

The barley nodded heavy-headed but unripening in the September fields. It wanted only a brief run of hot, dry days to make it ready for the combine – the twentieth century's scythe. The weather was not forthcoming.

Our rural friends studied the sultry skies willing the sun to appear, and walked into the thigh-high crop to gather handfuls of grain to roll on their palms and see whether it could be harvested. It was not ready and they grumbled and muttered about mildews and moulds and rots as lethal as the Black Death and prophesied doom and disaster for all of us.

These forebodings sent a chill right through to our bank account. Our five acres might not be much but it was vital to our solvency. Now that the grass was failing, feed bills were beginning to build up and our overdraft still carried nasty bruises from the previous batch.

Howard, our stocky friend, and his wife Dilys, trim in a town-going dress, came visiting, bringing a box of windfall apples from their orchard. They stayed for tea and he did the barley-grabbing act and tried to reassure us that all was not yet lost. But John and I steadfastly refused all comfort.

We were sewing sacks whilst waiting for the weather to improve. Many of the sacks which had held the previous year's crop had rotted, been torn one way or another, or holed by rats and mice. We sorted through the pile in the foodstore, putting the good in one heap, the repairable in another, and the useless in a third.

Our equipment consisted of a ball of thin twine, big sailmaker's needles and scissors. For some reason Shirley found our efforts hilarious, perhaps because we both had bandaged fingers and because we ended up with some very odd-shaped sacks as we cobbled, tied and stitched. Never mind, they would all hold grain.

However, even after our tailoring efforts I had to acquire another two dozen sacks to bring the usable up to the hundred required the previous year and provide a few extra – just in case.

The wretched, indeterminate weather stuttered and stumbled along until one hot day spawned a second, grew into a week and then lengthened, a little unsteadily, into an Indian summer. There was an unreal quality about the world in the early milking hours. It appeared to be in a state of suspended animation; the heavy atmosphere blanketed sound; the first crow flapping ragged, fingered wings seemed to swim, rather than fly over the fields; the dairy cows lay full-bellied and content, getting up only reluctantly to plod, single file, sleepily, to the milking parlour.

By mid-morning the mood had changed. The sun blazed, sucking up the moisture and the combines began to operate on farms around us. The quietly spoken Price, shirt-sleeved, with a worn leather belt gathering his trousers around his lean middle, came to check our crop and decide if it could be combined. He used his slow, easy smile as a foil against our impatience while he gathered samples of grain from different spots and pulled them to pieces with hard, long-fingered hands.

'It is ready,' he announced after proper deliberation. 'I'll come tomorrow afore dinner. Could you bring the tractor to my place and collect a trailer?'

We could indeed. John – jeaned and T-shirted – went off with the easy, swinging stride of youth unshortened by the years, and came back with the machine, ready to chase our visitor's car. I closed the gate behind them but in no time at all our son re-appeared, towing a big, four-wheeled grain trailer and positioned it, ready for use, in one corner of the barley field. There was nothing to do now except cross fingers and hope there would be no sudden, treacherous change in the weather or that anything else would go awry.

Nothing did go wrong. Mid-morning the next day, the four geese, headed by Moses our truculent gander, gave us warning that Price and his red-painted combine were on the way. The long-necked quartet always knew when a vehicle left the tar-macked road three-quarters of a mile away and started down the rough lane. Their hearing was more acute than the dogs' and their hair-raising cackle outdid any doorbell.

Half an hour later Operation Barley was under way. Perched

on a seat high above the intake rollers, Price steered the ungainly but efficient combine round the edge of the grain, cutting an eight-foot swathe like some super lawn-mower. The machine gathered in the barley, threshed it, and dumped the straw on the field while the fat kernels poured in a golden stream from a down-curving spout into the combine's tank.

When the gauges told him over two tons had been collected, Price pulled alongside the trailer and, swinging the feed spout over, transferred the grain. We promptly towed the trailer into the stockyard and engaged in a frenzy of bagging.

Shirley operated a handle to open a square-mouthed chute and send the grain cascading into the sacks John and I held open. We tied them with rough binder twine and used the two-wheeler trolley to lug them into the bottom end of the long foodstore to be kept until needed. This first batch produced forty-six bulging sacks.

The haste was necessitated by the need to have the trailer ready for the next load. It was managed with a few minutes to spare. A repeat performance produced another twenty-eight bags.

The third, and final, transfer came when all the crop had been cut. Price made his usual brief farewells and departed, leaving us to finish the bagging and return the trailer later.

It was heavy, back-aching work because, quite apart from the weight of the filled sacks, there were a number of awkward steps to drag the trolley up and over to reach the store. It was a relief when the last sack had been lugged in and we could see exactly what our five acres had produced.

There were 107 sacks. Accepting that some of them contained more than one hundredweight – and being a bit optimistic – we estimated the yield to be about twenty-five hundredweights an acre. Not high, perhaps, compared with lusher, easier land, but extremely satisfying for us.

Later in the year we would call in the local mobile grinder service to convert the barley into animal foodstuffs. The merchant supplied various ingredients to go in the mix including wheat and molasses and the stock loved the resultant sweet-smelling meal. They were not the only ones to appreciate it. The meal was stored in the granary and, judging by the feathered comings and goings throughout the winter months, we were feeding half the areas's bird population.

Three days later Price's red-haired brother came down and baled our barley straw. He was an amiable giant who worked happily as a farm labourer and grumbled mildly now about having to surrender part of his precious holidays to help Price who had ambitiously taken on more commitments than he could meet.

'As if I didn't get enough of this earning m'bread,' the big man grinned ruefully, sitting on the baler. His idea of the *dolce vita* was a holiday camp in North Wales. 'It don't matter not at all if it rains,' he explained. 'There's plenty for the kids to do 'uthout moving a yard outside.'

As the machine moved along, gobbling up the dry straw, turning it into compressed bales, the dogs followed, catching moles in the soft, disturbed earth. They got three that we saw. The velvet-coated burrowers squeaked and threatened with pink, open mouths when yanked from their shallow runs into the bright sunlight. But coping with earthworms was one thing, fending off a determined Jack Russell terrier was quite different and they were quickly finished.

'Dogs never eats'um,' the red-haired one said. 'Folks do say they tastes very bitter, but how does they know? When we was kids, Price and me, we'd catch them in traps. You'd to stretch the skins on a board and dry them in the sun. You might get a penny, sometimes as much as threepence on them. There was an old bloke that collected them but, of course, he's long dead and it's all nylon and stuff now.'

The Jack Russell's nose led him to a bigger hole dug among the barley roots. The earth flew wildly as he dug into it with his short, powerful forefeet and there was a squeal as a fair-sized, plump rabbit was dragged out.

John took over, lying down to reach and bring out another four rabbits, making it five to go into the freezer. Red Head laughed and patted the excited little dog and said, 'I'll warrant this'n don't owe you much for his keep.'

Our crop produced 251 bales which we collected with our two-wheeler trailer and used as the foundation of the rick we intended to build for winter use. It was not nearly enough for our needs, so we borrowed a tractor and his biggest trailer from Howard and collected another 800 bales from a farm about two miles away at five pence a bale. It was beautiful clean straw, more suited to feeding than bedding, and when the winter came we augmented the hay ration with a couple of bales of it. There was never any left in the racks.

Once the straw had been collected, the pigs were turned into the stubble. Big and little they foraged happily, rooting out all manner of revolting delicacies. In the evening most of them followed the urgings of their stomachs and came hurrying back when we rattled a feed bucket and called them. But there were a trio of absentees: Percy, our young boar, and the two senior sows were reluctant to call it a day.

I went out and bullied the boar towards the pens. It was not too difficult because he was such a good-tempered animal. It needed a little pushing to keep him on a proper course because his big ears flopped over his eyes and tended to blind him. Once or twice he tried to double back but was persuaded to keep going, and eventually, when he realized that the other pigs were probably eating his rations, he ran, squealing his greed and protests, to join them.

The two sows were more hardened cases. They were used to fending for themselves. We had jokingly called them after two of Shirley's friends, rather elegant ladies. Now I heard her herding the pair along, playing a game of make-believe, slapping their ample bottoms and telling them, with obvious relish, 'Come on you pigs. Move along Dorfie, hurry up Dorrie . . .'

There was another bonus from the barley. The stubble attracted flocks of wild pigeons. They were quick-eyed, suspicious birds and it was extremely difficult to get close enough to use a shotgun. But John contrived a hide with some straw bales and a green tarpaulin and lay in wait. His catch was gratefully received, feathered, drawn, and dropped into the farm's cavernous freezer.

His companion on these expeditions was always Peter the Jack Russell. The chunky little dog had only to see the shotgun brought out to begin bouncing around, electric with excitement, but once in the fields he was a disciplined and efficient hunter, invaluable in running down pigeons or anything else that might have been winged and in danger of being lost.

On one occasion, however, their partnership was threatened. Before a shot had been fired the terrier took off after a covey of partridge which promptly bulleted up and over the nearest hedge, landing almost immediately and scurrying away through the grass. There were some hot words from John, but these died when the dog reappeared carrying a partridge.

The bird had a broken wing which had prevented it flying with the covey. It was an old injury and the wound had healed but it was enough to ensure that the bird could not have escaped the winter predators; the red fox that worked the area would have nosed it out sooner or later. One question the incident raised was how the dog had been able to recognize the bird's vulnerability and know it could be run down. Normally he would wait for the shotgun to be fired before taking off to do his bit.

Summer had melted into autumn so insidiously that the takeover had almost escaped notice. The swallows gave it away. They began congregating on the telephone wires, in dozens, then scores, then hundreds, excited little birds waiting for some mysterious signal that would send them on their way.

We kept an eye on them throughout the day but still failed to see the takeoff, only becoming aware they had gone when we missed their twittering. By then they were already high above the farm climbing to join a flock that must have come down from further north, mere dots against a blue sky streaked with cirrus.

'They've gone south, in Africa, to spend the winter,' Nicholas, who had not gone to school for some reason, told us. 'They'll come back next year.'

'How will they know they've arrived wherever it is they're going?' I asked him facetiously.

'Their hearts will tell them,' he said with a child's wisdom.

There was a harvest thanksgiving service in a local church, not the nearest, but one we preferred because it was small and homely, secreted away in thick groves of yew trees, with no more than a dozen houses in the village. The clergyman was an old man, tall and stooping, with a gentle, contented face and tolerant eyes. He appeared unaware how rarely we appeared although there were seldom a score in his congregation.

The nave had been decorated with flowers, grasses and ever-greens. A long elm table set inside the arched doorway was covered with offerings of fruit, vegetables, pots of jam and honey. We added ours. The centrepiece of the whole was a great, home-baked loaf, moulded and plaited to resemble a sheaf of corn. Someone had cunningly twisted barley straw to make little, face-less dollies and rested them against the heaped plates.

Before the short service began – the old man did not favour long-winded sessions – there was a baby boy to christen. The tall farmworker father, uncomfortable in his best brown suit, handed over the child with work-hardened hands while his wife, a small, round-faced girl with large eyes, watched anxiously.

There was no cause for concern. The old man went lovingly through the service and then, departing from the set ritual, sud-denly lifted the baby high in the air above the watching family group. 'No wonder the good God loves them, they'm so beauti-ful,' he exclaimed, and then he kissed the child gently and handed it back to the relieved mother.

As we left the church someone touched my shoulder and I turned to see Old Jonathon with his brother Matthew. 'I didn't know you came here,' he said.

The clergyman was within earshot.

'Not often enough,' I said embarrassedly.

The old man extended his hand. 'You are always welcome.'

Jonathon was unabashed. 'This is our own church. We come here when we was boys and Mother was alive.' He indicated the straw dollies. 'See them, Jacky? If you'd one of them in the house, you'd have no bad luck for the next year. Ain't that so, Vicar?'

'So I've heard it said, Jonathon,' the tall man said smiling. 'But I don't know that I'd believe it.'

No one actually saw Chanticleer, our chauvinistic cockerel, take on the red fox – the wily old predator with the distinctive coat which worked our area – but the evidence at the scene suggested the sort of heroic conflict which inspired the ancient bards.

It took place in the barley field and was brought about because of an urge to scratch by our beef cattle, notably Ferdinand the red bullock, his friend, coal-black Taffy, and six others.

After the barley harvest the bunch were allowed into the Five-Acre to glean what they could and eat down the grass that had grown unchecked round the edge of the crop. They obviously found something tasty in the hedges too because we often saw them pulling at branches to reach leaves or tender shoots.

The henhouse occupied by Chanticleer and his two dozen wives was sited on a triangle of waste ground bordering the side of the field nearest the house. It was this which led to the confrontation.

Chanticleer, a handsome white bird with a glint of gold about him and impressive red plumes, numbered gamecocks among his ancestors. He had cost me exactly twenty pence at a sale and had been intended for the cooking pot. He was saved because the kids had a picture book with a cockerel hero, Chanticleer, which looked exactly like my acquisition. So, into the henhouse he went to play husband to two dozen hens, mainly Leghorns. A daunting prospect for any male but one he tackled with such gusto it brought out the Women's Libber in my wife.

The bullocks did not directly interfere with the cockerel and his retinue but they liked to rub against a sharp corner of the henhouse, presumably because it was more effective than the trees they usually favoured. They were heavy animals and it was this which had sprung the lock and let in the red fox.

It happened on a cold, still night lighted by a clear moon. I was asleep when the geese started their cackling and the dogs, particularly the Jack Russell, began to go berserk. The noise penetrated my sleep and I climbed, reluctantly, out of bed to investigate.

No chance of ignoring it and sleeping on. The last time such a commotion happened we found that one of the younger sows had managed to wedge her head between the metal bars of the sty door. It needed a crowbar to get her out.

I pulled on outdoor clothes, found wellingtons and anorak in the hall, and went out brandishing a big torch. First step was to loose the dogs from their pen. Peter the terrier shot towards the barley field as fast as his short legs could take him. The collie was more restrained; she ran, whining, in that direction but waited for me to say what should be done.

There was no sign of Peter when we arrived but the swinging, open door of the henhouse told the story. I went inside, dreading what might be waiting, expecting to find the place filled with feathers and bodies. Foxes, they say, will kill for the excitement if they get into a chicken run. But there were no dead birds here. They must have run for it when the intruder arrived. Perhaps they were already outside.

A few yards from the hut door I found the headless remains of a hen in the ditch. Nothing else until, lying on an open patch further into the field, I spotted Chanticleer. He was dead, badly torn about, but all the bits were there.

John arrived and stood shivering by me. 'That damned fox,' he exploded and walked across and picked up the still warm body.

'Well, what do you know? This old cock put up a fight,' he exclaimed. The bird's strong claws were thick with red fox hair and there were signs of the scuffle in the dust.

It was not too surprising. We had known the bossy cockerel send our own dogs and cats packing. It must have been his breeding. Perhaps it was the cockerel's challenge, however doomed, which had limited the fox's success. Probably Peter had arrived before any further damage could be done.

The bullocks came up to see what was happening. We drove them out of the field and closed the gate. Frightened hens were reappearing from hiding-places in hedgerow and ditch. Some must have simply headed into the open field because now they came running anxiously back.

We got nineteen of them into the shed, fastened it again and wedged a length of wood against the door for added safety. Any chickens still outside would have to take their chances of surviving until daylight. They did, in fact, get through what remained of the night safely.

There was no sign or sound of Peter so we left him to it, put the collie away and returned to bed. There were three hours' sleep before the alarm would go off.

The terrier came back when I was working in the milking parlour, wagging his stumpy tail and back-end, anxious to ingratiate himself. He was thick with mud which suggested an attempt to dig something out, presumably the fox, but there was no sign of blood so he did not appear to have succeeded. I slung him in with the collie and got on with the milking.

For some reason the incident awakened an undying hatred of foxes in the fierce little dog. If he came across a used earth, he would go down unless restrained. On one occasion he disappeared before anyone could prevent it. Nothing happened for some ten minutes but then all hell broke loose beneath our feet. It was a great relief when he reappeared, backwards, gory with the occupant's blood and very pleased with himself.

But it was not the red fox he had tackled in the earth. This was certain because one evening afterwards the dogs chased the distinctively coated fox across the top field and got so close the crafty animal ran up the sloping trunk of a hawthorn tree. He balanced there on the tangled branches while the terrier went almost insane trying to scrabble up to him.

John heard the commotion and went chasing down with the shotgun but there was no chance of a shot. He arrived in time to see the fox calmly tight-rope across a branch which stretched over the chain-link fencing dividing Egerton from a neighbouring farm and jump down to safety. He might not have thumbed his nose at his impotent pursuers, but his whole attitude did the job equally well as he trotted jauntily away.

27 The rams run out 🌹

Autumn had hung the hedges with berries and thrown a Joseph's coat over the hills. From the stubble where the barley had been I could see Shirley and the kids busy with baskets among the bushes and brambles down by the stream which marked Egerton's lower boundary.

These days the kitchen was stacked with jars and bottles, and the women of the family – Vicky was as enthusiastic as her mother – used their wooden spoons to stir seething messes in giant saucepans and assured us they would become delicious jams, jellies, syrups or cordials guaranteed to keep a person cold-free over the winter.

The place was continually filled with Shirley's friends, no-nonsense country ladies contemptuous of mere men who had never made cottage cheese, salted bacon or baked bread. Often they arrived with boxes of fruit – usually apples perfect for pulping and freezing in plastic bags – and carried away bags of sour crab-apples or bitter sloes. It looked a good trade to me.

From my vantage-point I could see the sheep inching their way across the field with the spring which the kids called 'Miracle' as they grazed. Behind me, in the top field, the cows were plainly visible. But, somehow, the farm felt empty. Perhaps it was because the hay and the barley were finished and the lambs had gone.

It was a Saturday; John had gone to play rugby for one of the local teams. We could expect him back about eleven o'clock, bruised and limping, but certain to recover in time for the next game.

There was an auction at The Forge so, although we had nothing to sell and did not wish to buy, I went back to the house, left a note of my intentions under a jar of damson jam, and walked up the lane to see what was happening. The willow-herb and cow-parsley had lost their battle with the season – and bowed their heads in defeat. The verges were tangled jungles of bracken, vetches, rushes and dying grass. A gaudy, aldermanic cock pheasant strutted across the track ahead until I shied a stone at him. It was a couple of yards off target but the bird cast aside his dignity and rushed for the hedge and safety. For some reason the incident lightened my mood.

The sale was all but over when I arrived. One of the final lots – three large framed but gaunt red beef animals – were in the ring and bidding was in full swing. A lot of possible buyers had already left and they were knocked down at £68 each to Jonas, the tall, drooping trader who came occasionally to The Forge pub for a beer.

It was a bargain price and Howard, our friend, on the far side of the buyer, snorted, 'Bare-faced robbery. They'm worth £10 apiece more.'

Jonas turned his sly-humorous face towards the shorter man. 'They'm yours at that price, Howard, if you wants them.'

But our stocky friend ignored the hand offered to seal the deal. 'No damn fear,' he said uncomfortably, and then, to me, glad to change the subject, 'You've missed just about everything. These was only some brought in late. The sheep's all gone.'

'I just came along to watch,' I explained.

'Never mind. Come and give us a hand to throw some little lambs I've got into the back of my pick-up. We need to talk about getting the rams out.'

Jonas listened to our mutual friend with a wry little smile on his face. 'See the two of you in the bar in a few minutes. There's a little business to be done.'

He went off and Howard, aware that he had been upstaged, said, 'He's so bloody sharp, he'll cut himself one of these fine days.'

The lambs he had bought for well under three pounds each were tiny, toylike creatures, more like ladies' purses than potential mutton chops. They were soon packed in and secured. 'You won't recognize them next spring,' he told me.

In the pub we greeted our friends and Griff leaned over his polished bar and said, 'Sunday, Jacky, the 26th. Last Sunday in the month.'

'What is?' I asked.

'Running out the rams, of course,' he said, pulling a tap handle to fill glasses for a thin, wiry man who was buying a big round for a rowdy group.

'Oh, the rams,' I said. 'Howard did mention it, I'd forgotten. That's fine with me. He's been keeping my ram at his place.'

It was important to coordinate the time when the rams were released into the ewe flocks to begin the breeding cycle again. Ewes come on heat every three weeks until they are in lamb. Small farmers like us changed rams with their friends so that if anything had gone wrong, say a ram was infertile, and the ewes came on again they would be served the second time by a sound male. It was sensible insurance. There were plenty of stories about infertile rams – a knock might do it.

Another point was that turning the rams out about the end of October meant lambs arriving about the end of March, when there was easier weather and new grass in the offing. If they came earlier in the year the weather would take a heavy toll unless they were kept inside. It was not unknown for newborn lambs to be frozen to the ground.

'That ram of yours has been running with a pair of mine in that little paddock up under the wood,' Howard said. 'They'm all as fit as fleas. I'll have him ready for you to collect the Sunday morning.'

Griff was drawing our beers when Jonas reappeared looking pleased with something he was at pains to hide. 'My treat,' he said, reaching over with a long, thin arm and putting a five-pound note on the bar. 'You have one as well, Griff.'

'How's you planning to get them stolen cattle down to your place?' Howard demanded.

'Cattle? Oh, you mean them three I just bought? They ain't mine now, Howard. Been sold to old man Hughes. He wants them to go in his yard over the winter.'

Just as he was aware it would, the news made Howard snort. 'You'm a great big crook, Jonas. I'll bet you took thirty pounds out of them beasts 'uthout doing a stroke of work.'

The dealer laughed at his indignation. 'Twenty-five pounds, Howard, I'm not a greedy man . . . and this is my work.'

I took a draught of beer to hide my smile and noticed that Griff was doing the same.

There was an urgency and excitement about the breeding flock as the old, primeval impulse possessed them. All the lambs had gone and the ewes were fat and fresh from the summer living, eager for the ram.

Early on the appointed Sunday John and I took the old van and went along to collect him. There was a tall, portly man with Howard when we arrived; one of his many relatives. We shook hands and chatted but afterwards I could not remember his name. Perhaps it had not been given.

The ram was ready, penned with Howard's two, in a dry, disused pig-sty. The four of us leaned over the low, red-brick wall and discussed the trio – all black-faced Suffolks. This was the lowland breed experience had taught the locals to cross with their own upland sheep to produce the blocky, meaty lambs butchers demanded.

All three animals were in fine condition but ours, perhaps because he was younger, looked the best.

'How many ewes have you got, seventy-odd?' Howard asked. 'This boy's good for twice that number. You done yourself a bit of good when you bought him.'

'They'm all three good rams,' the relative said. 'Not a bad one there. I'll tell you, Howard my boy, if the men was as good as their rams, there'd be a lot of very happy ladies round here.'

With four pairs of hands there was no difficulty getting the animal loaded.

'Don't forget to raddle him afore he's loosed,' Howard impressed on me. 'I shall use red, so you use blue, then we shall have a check when they'm swapped.'

I promised to do just that and off we went. Raddling meant smearing a colour compound on the ram's chest so that any ewe served was marked. It was easily done and afterwards, just as the previous year, we drove the van into the field where the flock was waiting. The rutting ewes smelled the male and crowded and shoved excitedly until we opened the rear doors and they saw the ram standing, looking down at them. Momentarily the whole lot froze. Then he jumped to the grass, the flock closed round him and they moved away from us.

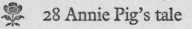

28 Annie Pig's tale

Right from the start Shirley was worried about Annie Pig's condition. There was something about the young pregnant sow – an acquisition in a trade deal – which triggered off an alarm deep in my wife's mind. Perhaps it was womanly intuition – a subject the family often teased her about – but, much more likely, it was simply evidence of the sympathy she had for any animal about to give birth.

There had been the odd hang-up with our sows and their litters but, we flattered ourselves, we had really done quite well and had succeeded in rearing a very high percentage. But as with everything else, there had to be an exception: ours was Annie.

One chilly October morning John and I came in from the bottom fields where we had been checking the sheep and found Shirley, jeaned and sweatered, leaning against the sty wall studying the sow which she had just fed.

'There's something I'm not quite happy about,' she told us, without being able to say precisely what inspired this opinion. 'She's too quiet . . . too docile.'

There seemed nothing wrong about the way the sow was eating.

Experience had imprinted us with the necessity of keeping careful records, noting just when sows went to the boar, when litters were due, and when the expectant pigs needed to be moved into the farrowing unit – 'the maternity hospital' the kids called it.

Four days prior to pigging we ushered them into the confining, tubular steel crates which were designed to prevent sows flopping on their newborn piglets with fatal results. In the crates the sows could stand comfortably but were not able to turn round, which also made it easier to look after them when they were giving birth.

Annie was due to produce on the twentieth of the month, but with eight days still to go John noticed that her dugs were tight with milk, normally a sign of fairly imminent birth. He climbed into the pen to check while the pig was distracted by some meal and sure enough, a tiny bubble of moisture – a watery milk substance – appeared on the end of a teat. If it was, indeed, the milk it appeared to be, we could expect the piglets to make their entrance into our farming world within the next twelve hours.

'You must have made a mistake in calculating,' he said accusingly as we cajoled and bullied the ungainly mother-to-be into a crate.

'It's hard to see how,' I told him defensively. 'The dates have been checked several times.'

He was unconvinced until, with the pig settled down, we took a quick look at the diary entries. The original dates appeared correct.

Shirley was not surprised. 'Haven't I been saying everything is not as it should be?' she demanded. 'I think she looks seedy.'

John and I began to get the same uneasy vibrations.

The next step was to activate the Holgate midwifery rota and Shirley, because of her interest in Annie, bravely offered to do the first graveyard stint. There was no need for her to repeat the offer. It entailed climbing out of bed about 2 a.m. and going down the dark, cold stockyard to check on the pig. That night I felt her leave my side and then, in spite of her cat creeping, woke again when she climbed back under the bedclothes.

'Not a sausage,' she said succinctly, turned over and promptly went to sleep.

Three hours later the alarm-clock bullied me out to begin the day's labours. There was no change: the pig opened her eyes but did not offer to move when I looked into the unit. That was rather disturbing because all the other sows always jumped up and demanded to be fed immediately in a manner becoming an animal about to add to the nation's pork and bacon stocks.

Broken nights were something we could manage without, but

we persisted because the rota system had led to us saving a number of piglets in the past – sometimes by extricating them from the afterbirth, occasionally by steering 'lost' piglets back to the warm sow and the infra-red lamp that hung over their creep area, and once by retrieving a little hog pig from a water trough it had managed to find and fall into after climbing over a low partition.

This time, though, our persistence was really tested because eight wearing days and nights went by before John came into the bedroom and quietly wakened me with the news that 'something' was happening. We would have let Shirley sleep on but she had no intention of being left out of things and joined us. By 4 a.m. Annie had produced nine piglets but that was the end of the good news. Shirley's premonitions were only too well justified.

The sow lay limp and exhausted, not able to rise and conjuring only a few half-hearted grunts to reassure the protesting, hungry litter pulling furiously at her teats and obviously not getting much.

There was only one thing to do: call in the vet. We did just that as soon as the clock showed a decent hour. His assistant, a slim, recently qualified young man, arrived, carried out a careful examination and pronounced, 'An infection of the uterus. I'll give her two injections now and leave another for you to give tomorrow. That ought to clear it up but I'm afraid she isn't likely to have much milk. You'll have to cope with the litter.'

That was not welcome news, especially for Shirley who invariably got landed with nursing sick and young animals, but there was no alternative. Soon after the vet's battered green Ford had disappeared up the lane, Shirley set off in the 1800, heading for the local Farmers' Cooperative to buy a sow milk substitute.

This life-saver mixed up into a rich, thick milk which had to be bottlefed to the ungrateful little wretches. They might well look like animated sausages, but they had voices like mini police sirens. And how they used them! The moment they were picked up they screeched fit to raise the roof. Normally such protests would have brought quick and fierce support but now the sow was too feeble to manage more than a few drawn-out sighs.

The three of us sat there holding struggling, protesting piglets on our knees and making like nursemaids with Indian tonic bottles – relics of palmier days – fitted with baby's bottle teats. It was a back-breaking, patience-sapping occupation, especially when it had to be done several times a day. It was a happy moment when the kids came charging down the lane from school, anxious to see the new babies, only too delighted to take over and help their mother.

Fortunately little pigs are quick learners, which was just as well because the milk was supplemented with a mixture which made up into a sad-looking grey gruel and this, at least in the beginning, had to be spoonfed to the curly-tailed brats. In fairness to them, they soon began slurping it up for themselves from a shallow enamel bowl.

Four days after giving birth the sow was still prostrate, refusing all solid food, and taking a mixture of glucose, milk and water only because we pushed a plastic funnel into the corner of her mouth and trickled the mixture down her throat.

'Hmm,' the young vet said after watching this operation. 'I don't much like the look of her, Mr Holgate.' That was a gross understatement as far as I was concerned.

Knowing the sick sow was lying there cast a gloom over the whole family. The depression thickened when the piglets began dying in spite of Shirley's coddling and caring. There were two dead one morning and a third went the following day. Looking at her face, I felt that the fates were being harsh and that this particular farmer's wife deserved better reward for her efforts.

Happily things began to improve. A week after her farrowing John pushed a bowl of fresh concentrates under the sow's nose and, surprisingly, she began to try and scramble to her feet. Everyone promptly abandoned all other activities and pushed and pulled to help her up. Finally we got a rope, padded it with a rolled sack, passed it under her and heaved like mariners trying to get a ship clear of the rocks. Everyone was breathless and sweating before there was a final effort by the pig and she balanced herself, weak and shaky but standing unaided. A few minutes later she was in sufficient control to bend her head to reach the sweet-smelling pig-nuts that had inspired the effort. We tiptoed out, afraid to speak until we were in the yard lest we distract her. Next morning the young vet was as pleased as us to see the improvement.

Even so several more days ticked by before Annie was judged strong enough to be moved into a follow-on pen and join her family. By now the piglets were independent and well able to fend for themselves.

When they were brought together we stood by in some trepidation, ready to intervene if she should reject them, but our fears were ill founded. The sextet of survivors ran round her excitedly, squealing and jumping to reach the dry, wrinkled dugs, and the sow sniffed them all and then lay down and stretched out, content to let them climb over her.

In all but feeding she was an excellent mother. The piglets would gobble up their food and rush back to her for warmth and protection. Really, the story should have a happy ending, but, like so many in farming, there could not be a wholly satisfying one.

We took the vet's advice and Annie never went back to the boar. Instead, when her pigs were sold as weaners at nine weeks old, she was moved into a smaller pen by herself and given all the food she could eat. But, alas, it was not done out of the kindness of our hearts. No, poor Annie was destined to be fattened and sold for the processed meat trade.

As for John and me; we determined in future to take Shirley's womanly intuition a little more seriously than we had in the past.

 29 A threadbare countryside

The leaves began falling, lying beneath the trees like coins scattered by some drunken profligate. November was with us. The countryside began to look rather threadbare and worn at the elbows and there was a bite in the milking morning air that had not been there a week or so before.

The mere thought of colder weather brought Shirley out in a rash of woollens. She began laying in stores of food and other essentials, packing the larder, filling shelves to groaning point.

'It's winter that's coming, not the end of the world,' I told her, but my wit was not appreciated.

'Better safe than sorry,' she declared smugly and marched about taking stock and making entries in an old ledger she had found somewhere. It read like a grocer's shop inventory.

A couple of brothers, short, hairy, beery fellows who lived on the far side of the mountain and owned a family coal pit – perhaps quarry is a better description – came down the lane in a rattle-trap of a lorry which threatened to fall to pieces, to see if we wanted to buy any. It was poor quality, slate-like stuff but it was coal and it was cheap. They were in a hurry to get back to The Forge before it closed and took £20 for their load, about a ton-and-a-half. They shovelled it into the outside coalhouse and hurried off to slake their increased thirst and rid their throats of the dust.

There were several of these little pits about the district. They were open-cast workings and unsuitable for commercial exploitation. Their owners used them as bank accounts, digging coal when extra cash was needed for holidays, school outings or something similar. Now, of course, it was for Christmas.

I had acquired a secondhand power-saw from an understanding merchant who was in no hurry to be paid. There were plenty of fallen trees about and John and I cut several trailer-loads of logs and stacked them ready for use. Shirley was quite effusive, but then the cheque arrived.

It was for £178 – payment of government subsidies on beef cattle – and I had very definite plans for it. So had she and that spelled trouble. 'Just about enough to buy a warm winter,' she declared, waving the cheque about.

Not so. It was going to buy a cow.

'So, who wants a smelly cow when we can be warm?' she demanded aggressively.

In my most dignified voice I informed her, 'I'm warm enough.'

'Where there's no sense, there's no feeling,' she said rudely.

I tried another tack. 'You may not have noticed, dear, but we don't have gas.'

'Don't you come the technical chauvinist with me, Farmer Giles,' she snapped. 'There are such things as oil and electricity.'

She really was in a bad mood. It seemed advisable to compromise, play for time. 'Oil is too expensive, electricity might be possible.'

'Really? Like storage heaters?'

'Something like that; I'll try and call in at the showrooms on Monday.'

She sprang the trap gleefully. 'Don't bother! I've got all the information we need. They've got a special offer. Free installation. Three heaters for £148. You can make a £50 deposit and pay the rest over three years. What do you think about that?'

'It sounds reasonable.'

'I'm so glad you think so,' she said, opening the sideboard drawer and producing a form. 'Just put your great big chauvinistic signature here. I've filled in the rest. They're coming on Friday to do the wiring.'

A man must know when to retreat. There seemed little to be gained by continuing to struggle. 'What about another cow?'

'Buy all the cows you want, be my guest,' she said all sweetness and light, and handed over the cheque. 'Only don't buy one costing more than £128 because £50 of this is being invested indoors for a change.'

It was easy enough to appreciate her point of view. Picturesque the house might be, but in winter it could get cold enough to freeze icebergs if the fires were not kept on at night. There was also, I had to admit, a tendency on my part to think 'outside' when any spare cash became available. I could only plead in defence that in the harsh weather, when the wind knifed round the mountain like a Welsh assassin, the house always seemed a haven of warmth and comfort beyond improvement.

Even so there were a few taut moments between us until the

heaters were installed. About a week after that had been done Shirley dragged me into the dining-room to see how the damp which worked up the two outside walls had been dried out. The satisfaction she derived from this was ample justification for the outlay. A lot of her predecessors at Egerton would, undoubtedly, have nodded approval of her militancy.

But the episode of the heaters was merely a family skirmish in the face of a steady advance by winter. Like everyone around us we got busy preparing for the siege.

One urgent task was to overhaul the hay racks – wooden-framed and welded wire mesh – and get them into position along one wall of the big cow yard where the herd would spend the winter. They had been taken down to allow easier access to the adjoining barns during haymaking.

It was just as well the racks were strongly made because soon after they had been fixed I slipped on a loose bale and fell some ten feet into them, landing with a breathtaking thump, bruised and shaken but unharmed and happy not to have gone all the way to the ground. I climbed out feeling very sorry for myself and limped into the house to beg a cup of tea.

Most things were somewhere near ready when I met Willem, our nearest neighbour, in the lane. He was in overalls, using a brushhook to cut back overhanging branches. 'They'm catching at the cars,' he explained, pausing to whet the crescent moon-shaped blade with a stone. 'Better get it done before the snow comes and brings the hedge all down into the lane. It's on the way and fast and early this year.'

'It?'

'Weather,' he explained patiently, nodding towards the north-east where the sky looked seasick. 'There's a mountain of snow up there. Likely this lane'll be filled to your shoulders.'

I was glad Shirley was not present. She would have had night-mares.

'It' came three days later but, fortunately, after a warning. The temperature dropped suddenly in mid-afternoon, there was a flurry of fine snow, and the land held its breath and waited. John and I were busy mending fences, we put away our tools and went to bring the cows in for the night for the first time. They needed no persuasion; they were even better prophets than the pessimistic Willem. It began snowing before we went to bed and next morning we woke to a cottonwool world.

Not everyone was prepared. When I went up the lane with the milk and got down to open the gate, I noticed a small, round-eyed owl, perhaps six inches high, perched unhappily in a hawthorn fork. We looked steadily at each other for a minute or so and then he lurched out and flew down towards Egerton's buildings, only to be mobbed by sparrows made brave by their numbers. Probably he had taken refuge in the hedge when it began to snow. We were used to the sound of screech owls hunting at night but very rarely saw the birds.

When little Jock arrived he shrugged off our neighbour's pessimism. 'This'll change to rain,' he said and was right. It soaked down solidly for three days, reducing the fields to porridge and the lane to a muddy hill-climb. Willem, John and I worked with pick and shovel to drain off the worst pools and keep the lane open. The damp and the work aggravated my arthritic hip and back but it had to be done.

There was no sympathy though from Matthew, a fellow sufferer. 'You'm catching me up quickly,' he teased when I walked into The Forge and sat down gingerly in a chair. 'Next show we shall have to have a crutch race.' Had there been such an event that night he would have won.

Happily the weather improved towards the end of November and Thomas, Ellis the Cowman's son-in-law, was able to plough the Five-Acre for us. Frosts and snow would break down the upturned earth so that when spring came round again we would have no difficulty working it down to the fine tilth we needed for the grass seed we intended to sow.

Thomas was in his usual good health and spirits when he joined us in the kitchen. 'You'm both invited to our television party next Saturday,' he informed us as we ate a very late lunch. 'We'm going to watch Match of the Day.'

It seemed a little strange.

'There's a television in the next room,' I pointed out.

He paused with a forkful of potato in mid-air. 'Black and white, ours is coloured.'

Shirley was impressed. 'You must be doing well, Thomas, to have colour TV.'

'We ain't bought it,' he laughed, showing strong white teeth.

'Hire purchase?'

He finished his potato. 'Not exactly, it's on approval. No deposit. Free trial in your own home, fourteen days, no strings . . .'

'Then?'

'Then they comes and takes it back,' he grinned happily. 'We've always wanted colour telly, me and the missus. Ellis likes it too. But the prices, they'm city prices, shocking.'

Shirley scurried from the room holding a hand over her mouth. I stayed in control until our guest added matter of factly, 'Mind, we'd rather 've 'ad it over Christmas, better programmes, but they wouldn't agree. They'm not a very helpful lot.'

When I laughed he joined in.

'First colour telly round here, y'know. Me and Ellis is setting the pace.'

'Introducing a touch of culture?' I suggested.

He grinned. 'I'll tell him you said that, but don't forget now, come on Saturday if you wants to see it. Likely enough it'll be gone next week.'

And off he went on his heavy tractor, driving with all the dash and thrust of the racing motorists he idolized.

We never took up the invitation but the incident certainly brought a little colour into our lives at a moment when it was much appreciated.

 30 A ewe is killed by dogs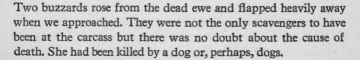

Two buzzards rose from the dead ewe and flapped heavily away when we approached. They were not the only scavengers to have been at the carcass but there was no doubt about the cause of death. She had been killed by a dog or, perhaps, dogs.

John and I stood looking at the mess spread around the area where the slaughter had taken place while Peter, the terrier, sniffed suspiciously at the dead animal.

The killers had long since gone, but what other damage had been done? We set out to search the gulleys and were relieved when it appeared there was only the one victim. The rest of the flock were grazing unconcerned on the snow-covered field.

'There'd have been at least one lamb in the spring,' my son said after a closer examination. 'I'd like to get a shot at whatever did it.'

So would I, but there was little likelihood of it happening. What we had to worry about now was how many unborn lambs might be lost as a result of the harrying of the flock. It was something only time could tell.

It was a good December day with the ground iron-hard and powdered with snow, and air as invigorating as chilled wine. Much, much preferable to the rain we had been experiencing. Nothing could be more depressing than walking around in damp clothes, although, after prolonged nagging by Shirley, we had bought waterproof working jackets and over-trousers which kept us much drier.

Sheep-worrying was a constant concern and there were persistent local reports of stray dogs. Just the previous week a mysterious Alsatian running with a collie-type dog had appeared in our top fields, making for the flock. Fortunately the kids spotted them and raised the alarm. John went off with the shotgun but the intruders saw him coming, turned tail and ran. He fired in their direction but they were well out of range.

It was a disturbing incident and one that kept us on tenterhooks for the next few days. The slightest unusual sound at night had me awake and worrying, trying to figure what it was.

Now we had lost this ewe. Was it the same dogs? Several characters in The Forge had spoken of similar incidents.

'Likely they'm sitting in front of someone's bloody fire by now,' Matthew said, shifting his weight in the chair to ease his back. 'They'm coming and going from somewhere, that's for sure. We'd summat like this a few years back; three damn great dogs running wild and killing all over the place. In the end we'd to get together and hunt them down but it took the best part of a week before the last one was buried. They never had owners, the like of these never do, not anyone who'll stand up and say so, anyway.'

'Well, they ain't townees' dogs this time of the year, there's none of them around,' someone else said.

Our insurance agent accepted a claim for £18 on the strength of a corroborating statement signed by Willem, our nearest neighbour, who walked over and inspected the carcass.

'I hope this ain't the start of what Matthew was on about,' he said lugubriously. 'There's space enough round here to lose a hundred dogs.'

He was right. The two of us stood together studying the country which stretched away, climbing steadily until it finally swept up to the mountain. The bare thorn hedges of the white, irregular fields looked like pencil marks, the leafless trees stood in dark, secretive groves or else singly, isolated, alone, stark and beautiful. Three black crows flew along the line of the gulley and Willem suddenly quoted the kids' rhyme. 'One for sorrow, two for joy, three for a letter . . . You'm going to hear from somebody far off, Jacky.' It was difficult to guess whether he was serious or joking.

That afternoon John and I dragged the mangled carcass to the rough ground fringing the stream and managed, using picks as well as spades, to dig a hole big enough to cover it. The operation left a low mound and the kids, who had come along to watch, fashioned a rough cross of dead branches and stuck it into the ground at one end.

'Better than ending up in meat pies, I suppose,' John commented, referring to the fact that aged sheep sold in the market – 'slaughter ewes' – mostly went to the processed meat trade.

It was approaching Christmas when a little dark-haired man, Mervyn, who had a farm across the valley from us and ran milking cows, came and stood quietly by me during an auction sale. We had something of the friendship shared by all men who work with their hands and make their living the same way.

'I heard you'd had trouble with dogs.'

'We lost a good ewe and her lamb a couple of weeks ago.'

He nodded sympathetically, his eyes on the cattle that were being sold. A little smile played at the corner of his mouth.

'Big Alsatian and a collie bitch?'

His words made me turn to look at him but his own eyes were steadily on the ring.

'Might well have been. Those two were running over our place a few days before it happened but took off when we went after them.'

'You won't see them again,' he said simply.

'Positive?'

'Positive. We'd three good sheep killed the week afore last. Right across the valley from you.'

Neither of us spoke for half a minute, then he laid a finger alongside his nose, counselling discretion. 'They do say old Tom Collier that farms t'other side of the brook 'as got no dogs around his place. If you knows someone with a good pup, he might be interested.'

He went off to rejoin his cronies, leaving me with mine.

'What's he want?' Howard asked.

'Nothing. Just passing the time of day.'

 # 31 The eve of Christmas and a calf

Christmas was coming! The kids were learning carols and Shirley was baking mince-pies for the party which, this year, was to follow the school choir service. The house was scented with mouth-watering smells. By now I knew all the words of 'O Come, All Ye Faithful'. In my own childhood we must have been content with the first verse because that was all I could remember; perhaps I had simply forgotten the rest.

The service was a local 'must'. There were a number of muddied, battered Land-Rovers in the school yard when we arrived, suggesting that we were not the only ones to live at the end of a rough, unsurfaced lane.

The school was functional, red-brick Victorian redeemed by lovingly tended gardens, spotless paintwork and that indefinable feeling that goes with a happy place. Inside it was draped with homemade coloured paper chains and cut-out bells. The oxen in the nativity tableau looked suspiciously like Herefords and the sheep were definitely Clun Forest.

No choir – all the school's forty pupils were in it – could have hoped for a better audience. Mums in best dresses, clear-eyed, not one hair out of place; Dads in sensible tweed suits, highly polished boots and ill-knotted ties; younger brothers threatened with instant destruction if they did anything awful; and pretty, Sunday-dressed, lipsticked older sisters trying furtively to catch the eye of someone else's older brother and looking down demurely when they succeeded.

The spinster headmistress tapped her knitting needle baton on the music stand, the other half of the staff, the twenty-two-year-old, gave her attention to the piano, and the choir launched into a rendering of 'The Holly and the Ivy' that made the windows rattle.

Our pair were well to the fore. All our suffering and their practice was justified. Vicky sang the solo verses of the final piece, 'O Come, All Ye Faithful', in a sweet, true voice and Nicholas, as uninhibited as ever, was louder even than the previous year, benefiting from lungs developed by chasing over Egerton's hilly fields.

When it was over and the applause had been acknowledged, the party began. The choir swooped like locusts. Shirley's three dozen mince-pies disappeared in a twinkling. Nicholas's chums agreed that she was an excellent cook and invited him to sample their own families' contributions. By the time we took our leave, he was so full his eyes were bulging.

The weather made no concessions to the festive season. It was bitterly cold but it was dry which made it endurable. The ground was hard enough to take the cows' weight without cutting up. We allowed them out after milking most mornings and they wandered about, pulling at the dead grass, melting the snow which covered it with the breath from their distended nostrils. When, as the light began to fade, we brought them in, they left clear, lozenge-shaped patches in the snow-spattered fields where they had been lying.

In the bottom acres the sheep came running to the wooden troughs, eager for the meagre ration of meal we brought. It was barely a couple of mouthfuls each but it helped them fend off the hardest weather. There was hay in the long, mobile rack but they preferred the grass which they reached by scraping away the snow with their forefeet.

We still had cattle out. Ferdinand, the red calf, Taffy, his black-coated friend, and six other bullocks were going to winter outside unless the weather deteriorated too much. They had grown thick coats and were fat and little bothered by the elements. We put hay in a free-standing rack with access from all four sides, but they preferred to use just two and jostled and pushed like boisterous schoolboys.

Their ration of concentrates was one bucketful a day. The sight of it arriving was sufficient to start a stampede and, as they were not fitted with brakes and so could not always stop when they wished, there was a real danger of being run down and trampled.

Everyone quickly learned to dump the concentrates and retreat because to dally was to risk being mobbed once the trough was emptied. They came charging up, trying to get their heads into the bucket, convinced it must still hold food. Since they weighed about six hundredweight, an affectionate nudge was sufficient to send a person sprawling . . . and it did, on several occasions.

All the locals were busy trying to cash in on the seasonal trade. Many of the wives raised poultry, getting the day-old chicks in July and selling them, fat and oven ready, for the Christmas tables.

This farmer's wife had not done that but our Yuletide dinner, a handsome stag turkey, was parading round the stockyard, gobbling and bullying the chickens. He was one of two survivors – the other was a smaller hen turkey – of three tiny poults Shirley had bought for twenty-five pence each in the summer. When he

168

finally appeared in his ultimate role, he weighed fifteen pounds.

The kids were full of festive spirit. They scoured the farm to find enough berried holly to decorate the house and spent long, happy hours making paper chains and dressing a Christmas tree to stand in a corner of the main living-room.

When Shirley and I walked up to The Forge one evening, Old Jonathon bought us drinks and asked her, 'Do you have any mistletoe?'

His friends cheered and she played up to them and said, 'Jonathon . . . and I didn't know you cared!'

'No, no,' he protested. 'I meant if you want some there's a big bunch on an apple tree in my garden.'

'Perhaps I'd better come and collect it,' I said. 'It would be tempting fate to leave you two alone, by the sound of things.'

Griff, always the perfect host, came to the old man's rescue. 'There's to be a bit of a sing-song the Eve of Christmas, the darts club is organizing something and little Taffy Beniams with the crooked leg from over at Nelson is bringing his melodeon. You'm both more than welcome.'

In the end the kids collected the mistletoe.

On the Eve of Christmas – to borrow Griff's words – a Sunday, we drove to the little church among the yew trees for morning service. The tall, elderly vicar with the gentle face preached a quiet, reverential sermon about the nativity in homely terms which made me think it had taken place on one of the local farms. It held the children – others as well as ours – spellbound. Afterwards he stood at the door, shook hands and remembered our family from Harvest Thanksgiving.

'Come back before Easter,' he told us with a smile.

We schemed to make our Christmas Day as trouble-free as possible. The experience gained the previous winter stood us in good stead. Getting the tractor or Old Lil, the diesel van, thawed out and running in time to get the milk up the lane for the morning collection was a recurring problem. So, rather than risk that happening on the day, we took the churns up after the evening milking and left them overnight to be collected. No chance of the milk going off in these temperatures. It meant being able to loaf in bed until 6 a.m. or even later for at least one day.

By seven o'clock on Christmas Eve everything had been done. The fire was crackling merrily with a mixture of oak logs and slate coal, we had eaten and cleared away, I was enjoying a glass of Shirley's purple elderberry wine and getting into the Santa Claus mood. Then John, who had gone for a final look round the stock, padded in on stockinged feet and asked me. 'That cow, the last one we got, know her?'

I did. She was a weary old creature heavy in calf who had come cheap because no one else, except the butchers, wanted her and they were not prepared to bid more than £94.

'She'll calve tonight!'

It was a bombshell exploding all over our carefully laid plans.

'You must be wrong,' I said hopefully. 'According to the AI certificate, she isn't due to calve before the end of next month.'

'Somebody must have made a mistake. Probably she took with the first insemination, came on bulling again, falsely, and they had her served again and that's the date on the certificate.'

It was feasible. I had heard of it happening.

'But tonight!'

The seventeen-year-old grinned. 'Come and see for yourself. I've brought her into the empty pen and strawed it.'

I put on a quilted anorak and wellingtons and went.

The cow was pulling phlegmatically at the hay in the wall rack but the light from the naked bulb was sufficient to show the trace of slime on her hindquarters. She had started calving! A few choice swear words escaped my lips.

'We were going to The Forge for a couple of hours.'

'You can still go,' John said. 'I'm not coming, I know where you are, and if nothing goes wrong, neither of us is needed.'

It was true: we settled for that arrangement.

It was gone nine o'clock when we parked the car and went into the pub. It was jam-packed full. No sooner were we through the door than our friends claimed us. 'C'mon, Jacky, cheer up,' fat Aaron from up the mountain said, thrusting a full tankard into my hand. 'Christmas tomorrow, peace on earth. You've got a face like the wheel fell off the cart.'

He looked quite 'posh' in a good suit, shirt actually buttoned across his chest and a tie, although the knot had worked round almost under his ear. This sartorial elegance was explained by the presence of his well-fleshed wife, Ria, who had made room for Shirley to sit next to her.

'Good Gawd,' Old Jonathon, neat and tidy in his 'Edwardian' suit and high winged collar, exploded when I told them about the calf. 'There's nothing any of us can teach that old girl. Sit back there and enjoy yourselves. Nothing like these in London, I'll be bound.'

There certainly was not as far as I was aware. 'These' were the Darts Club Glee Singers, six beer-podgy gents complete with barbers' aprons and false black moustaches. They were backed by a pianist and two straw-hatted, blazered banjo players. Mostly they sang nostalgic 1920s numbers and popular carols and did so very well, even if the hospitality was beginning to overwhelm their musical abilities. No one minded the odd lapse and when they forgot their words the audience simply took over.

The star of the evening was Little Taffy Beniams with his melodeon or, as Aaron persisted in calling it, his 'squeezebox'. He proved to be a man of considerable vintage and he sang country ditties that I had never heard before. Some were amusing, some were bawdy, and a few were strangely evocative of a way of life long gone.

It was all very enjoyable but I had the cow on my mind. So, with matters still going strongly, we made our farewells over protests, wished the whole house a Merry Christmas, and left.

The night was cold under a sky blanketed with light cloud, frost sparkled on the road and the hedges and verges were white with snow. When we turned into the lane the headlights picked up a rabbit and transfixed the creature until I flicked a switch and set it free.

John appeared from the stockyard at the sound of the car. 'Trouble,' he said simply. 'This calf's stuck. I'd have had him by now except he's got a leg twisted.'

I went indoors and changed back into working clothes. The clock above the fire said it was ten minutes to eleven.

The cow was securely neck haltered with a chain to a post. I stripped to my vest, soaped hand and arm, and felt for the calf.

One leg was indeed horribly twisted, lying under the animal's body and preventing the birth. It felt immovable.

For some twenty minutes we worked and tried to think how to correct it. Shirley came down the yard. 'Griff is on the telephone. Do you need help?' It was asking a bit to bring our celebrating friends down the lane at this hour. I went up to talk to him.

'Listen carefully,' he said after hearing of our lack of success, and proceeded to explain, step by step, what needed to be done. I promised to call back if there was any further need. 'I'll be here,' he said. 'Don't you hesitate.'

Down in the pen we began again. First step was to push the calf back in to make room to work. It sounded easy enough but the exertion of getting it done brought me out in sweat before, slowly, slowly, the calf moved. Step number two was to manipulate the knee joint. Slowly, gently, I inserted my hand, flat against the calf, until I felt the joint and was able to hook two fingers round it. A steady, maintained pull brought it forward and made it hinge and double. Finally, Griff had said to bring the forefoot into the proper birth position whereby hoofs and nose appear together. Again, there was an initial resistance but, finally, it was done. The relief made my hands tremble.

'We may still need to pull him,' John said, but it proved unnecessary. Fifteen minutes later it was all over. The cow's convulsions, which had almost ceased, began again and this time I was able to take the calf's forefeet and help. In the end the poor, long-suffering creature that had stood all my fumblings with the minimum of protests, groaned and made a supreme effort and the calf slithered to the straw bedding of the pen.

It was a small black and white heifer. For one moment she looked lifeless but then John bent and cleared her mouth and nose of mucus and she gasped.

'She's about exhausted,' he said.

I knew how she must feel.

The cow, restricted by the neck chain, twisted anxiously to try and reach the limp little animal. We carried the calf within her reach and stood back as the rough, life-bringing tongue went to work. The newcomer's breathing was spasmodic at first but soon began to settle into a regular rhythm.

'We're not wanted here now,' my son said.

He was right. We removed the restricting chain and went, leaving the light on.

Shirley was speaking to Griff on the phone when we walked in. 'All finished,' I told him, taking over. 'A little heifer calf. How are things going up there?'

'They'm all gone,' he said. 'Just me and the Missus doing the washing up. It's one o'clock, y'know. Happy Christmas.'

'And to you,' I said and hung up.

My wife was making coffee. It smelled delicious.

'What about Father Christmas?' I asked when she carried in a tray.

'He's been and gone, couldn't wait,' she smiled. 'I'll run some water for you to have a quick dip before we go to bed.'

John had washed in the kitchen sink. He took his mug and went upstairs, wishing us a wry goodnight.

The events of the last few hours had been rather shattering. I was still in a soiled vest, getting very chilled, and conscious of being unwashed. The coffee tasted like nectar. I drank it slowly without sitting down and looked round the room with its white-painted walls, beams, paper chains, lopsided, homemade Chinese lanterns, and tinsel-festooned tree.

'Christmas in the so-and-so country,' I said, feeling very sorry for myself.

Shirley laughed – a slim, pretty woman in a blue woollen dressing-gown. 'It's what we wanted. Happy Christmas, Farmer Giles.'

'Happy Christmas, wife,' I said.

Edward Vernon
Practice Makes Perfect 85p

Out in the waiting room lurk a confused old lady, a timid vet, a puzzled diabetic, a lonely housewife, a hypochondriac athlete, a tipster with an ulcer, a nun with dandruff, and a persistent young lady with abundant charms and perfect health!

Inside the surgery there is the general practitioner, filling out countless forms, outwitting the pill-freaks, destroying indestructible plastic syringes, watching pharmaceutical salesmen fill his office with gimmickry, and dreading the small hours phone call from a patient with a hangover!

'An entertaining and often hilarious look behind the surgery door . . . make a bedside book of it' DAILY TELEGRAPH

David Taylor
Zoovet 75p

The drowning Hippo . . . the arthritic Giraffe . . . the Killer Whale with ulcers . . . all just part of a day's work for the flying animal-doctor whose missions of mercy take him to Loch Ness, Arabia and Red China, as he answers cables from zoos, circuses and wildlife parks across the globe.

'Good humour and abounding energy on every page' WASHINGTON POST

'Wildly funny' SUNDAY MIRROR

Leslie Thomas
Some Lovely Islands 75p

'A travel book with a difference . . . Leslie Thomas has had a life-long yen for the remoteness and mystery of small islands. Writing with an enormous sense of fun and an eagle eye for off-beat detail, he describes his visits to ten tiny islands dotted around the British coast' DAILY EXPRESS

James Herriot
All Things Bright and Beautiful £1.50

This second omnibus takes up the story of the world's favourite vet
from the closing chapters of *All Creatures Great and Small*. James is now
married and living on the top floor of Skeldale House. He's a partner in
practice and his day is well filled with the life of a country vet, bumping
over the Dales in his little car en route to a host of patients from
farm-horses to budgerigars . . .

'Absolutely irresistible . . . told with warmth, charm and never-flagging
good humour' EVENING NEWS

Vets Might Fly 80p

A severe case of World War Two takes James Herriot away from his
vet's life in the Dales and into a training camp somewhere in England . . .

'There are funny cases, sad cases, farm animals and pets, downright
dialect-speaking farmers, ladies of retirement, hard-bitten NCOs and
of course the immortal Siegfried and Tristan' SUNDAY TIMES

Vet in a Spin 80p

Strapped into the cockpit of a Tiger Moth trainer, James Herriot has
swapped his wellingtons and breeches for sheep-skin boots and a baggy
flying suit. But the vet-turned-airman is the sort of trainee to terrify
flying instructors who've faced the Luftwaffe without flinching. Very
soon he's grounded, discharged and back to his old life in the dales
around Darrowby.

'Marks the emergence of Herriot as a mature writer'
YORKSHIRE POST

'Just as much fun as its predecessors. May it sell, as usual, in its millions!'
THE TIMES

Farley Mowat
The Boat Who Wouldn't Float 75p

'Never buy a boat of unknown ancestry . . . *Happy Adventure* was just
that, a schooner which leaked like a colander. It kept Farley Mowat a lot
in harbour and the people he introduces us to in the small Newfoundland
fishing ports are a rugged, independent, eccentric breed'
DAILY TELEGRAPH

'Farley Mowat is a brilliant writer' JAMES HERRIOT

The Dog Who Wouldn't Be 70p

The story of Mutt . . . his pedigree was uncertain but his eccentricity
was indisputable. He climbed trees and ladders, rode passenger in an
open car wearing goggles . . . Farley Mowat's best loved book tells the
richly entertaining story of the dog who owned him in the years of his
boyhood on the Canadian prairies.

'Transported me effortlessly to the heart of that wild, untamed country'
JAMES HERRIOT

You can buy these and other Pan Books from booksellers and
newsagents; or direct from the following address:
Pan Books, Sales Office, Cavaye Place, London SW10 9PG
Send purchase price plus 20p for the first book and 10p for
each additional book, to allow for postage and packing
Prices quoted are applicable in the UK

While every effort is made to keep prices low, it is sometimes
necessary to increase prices at short notice. Pan Books reserve
the right to show on covers and charge new retail prices which
may differ from those advertised in the text or elsewhere